SUCCESS FROM
BEING
MAD

Inspiring real life stories of
ten mad veterans of the Indian armed forces
who successfully carried
their madness to the entrepreneur world

I0490489

VETERAN COL RS SIDHU

INDIA · SINGAPORE · MALAYSIA

Notion Press

No. 8, 3rd Cross Street
CIT Colony, Mylapore
Chennai, Tamil Nadu – 600004

First Published by Notion Press 2020
Copyright © Veteran Col RS Sidhu 2020
All Rights Reserved.

ISBN 978-1-64951-705-0

This book has been published with all efforts taken to make the material error-free after the consent of the author. However, the author and the publisher do not assume and hereby disclaim any liability to any party for any loss, damage, or disruption caused by errors or omissions, whether such errors or omissions result from negligence, accident, or any other cause.

While every effort has been made to avoid any mistake or omission, this publication is being sold on the condition and understanding that neither the author nor the publishers or printers would be liable in any manner to any person by reason of any mistake or omission in this publication or for any action taken or omitted to be taken or advice rendered or accepted on the basis of this work. For any defect in printing or binding the publishers will be liable only to replace the defective copy by another copy of this work then available.

Contents

· ·

PART III.   INTERNATIONAL PERSPECTIVE

PART IV.   EPILOGUE

Foreword

. . . .

"SUCCESS FROM BEING MAD" is a book with an idea whose time has come. The title appears a bit misleading as it narrates stories of ten armed forces Veterans who have carried forward their passion of the service days (their madness) to the entrepreneur sector and excelling in ventures where they have no previous experience. The book speaks selectively and anecdotally of their early life, experiences within the armed forces, their corporate venture(s) and learnings from their experiences from the perspective of guiding new entrants into the field of entrepreneurship. Their stories highlight the positive aspects of the Armed Forces and the country as whole and the bright future awaiting the next generation of entrepreneurs.

The armed forces have traditionally been type cast in the public eye for their death and glory battlefield stories. In a similar vein the long held view in the corporate sector has been to best employ the Armed forces veterans as Security/Admin/HR managers. The book breaks this mould and draws focus of the industry towards leadership capabilities of the Armed Forces Veterans and their vision for a new and vibrant India of tomorrow.

Indian economic activity is already abuzz with innovative technological startups. The veterans from the Indian Armed Forces are suitably equipped with technical talent, leadership experience and undimmed passion to lead the Indian corporate charge into new horizons. The business leaders are masters of their own destiny, an idea befitting the veteran corporate warriors. Next gen veterans need to explore the entrepreneur route in larger numbers.

The learnings highlighted in the rich and varied entrepreneurship roles profiled in the book makes it a must read even for the aspiring young entrepreneurs emerging from our fine academic and business institutions. It has an excellent compilation of the desired qualities for entrepreneurship. There is a lot which can be learnt by the young generation aspiring to chart a new course of their own.

The author Col RS Sidhu has the right credentials to write on the subject. He has served in the army for 29 years, is a decorated soldier having been awarded the Sena Medal for gallantry. Post retirement he has worked in the Corporate Life Skills & Leadership Training/Education/ Hospitality sectors for more than a decade. Though this book is his maiden venture into the field of book writing, his predictive analysis on events and strategic matters have been published in magazines and journals of repute.

General (Dr) VK Singh, PVSM, AVSM, YSM (Retd)
Minister of State for Road Transport and Highways,
Government of India, New Delhi

Apologies as Preface

· ·

SUCCESS FROM BEING MAD showcases the power of passion in achieving success in life. It is your Passion which makes Happiness and Work inclusive and complementary to each other.

The aim of this book is not to belittle any person, organisation, profession, ethnicity, caste, religion, country or region. In case I have unwittingly hurt the emotions, feelings, pride, self-respect and beliefs of any being, in writing this book, I sincerely offer my deepest apologies.

There may be "*Madder*" profiles than those incorporated herein. So I also offer my apologies to the "Mad Vets" who could not make it to my selection of the "*Karma Yogis*." The reason is plain and simple. I have not come across your madness. So it is attributable to my ignorance and is my loss for missing out an interesting success story. If you still wish to take umbrage, well so be it.

Special Thanks: I Owe It To Them

My ability to write this book reflects the grooming, seasoning and hardening in the folds of three of the finest Mechanised Infantry Battalions of the Indian Army.

To 7 PUNJAB, now 8 MECH INF, the unit I was commissioned into. I could not have asked for a better entry into the army way of life. Unsurpassed professional élan, maximum opportunity to learn the profession, well-meaning mistakes taken in stride, fiercely protective of their own, and full encouragement to enjoy life outside the working hours. The Seven Second Punjabis, as I still fondly refer to the Paltan, are the happiest "happy-go-lucky" outfit.

To 15 MECH INF, the First Born as they are wont to call themselves and came to be known as "Mechanised Commandos" during raising. It became the first Mechanised Infantry Battalion to conduct amphibious operations overseas and to be actively deployed in counter-insurgency role. The wealth of combat experience earned therein, as a young leader, will not be easily duplicated.

To 12 MECH INF (8 PARAS 16 MAHAR), the unit with the reputation of being the most daring even in the never-say-die "Men Apart Every Man an Emperor" Paratrooper fraternity, both on and off the sports field. Irreverent to authority except for proven mettle, no task was insurmountable, whether arranging helicopters for on-the-quiet freefalls or tractor-trolley-based essential vehicle columns for planned cross border operations. The PARA MAHARS are the original, true blue, Mad Breed and happy to be known as such. It was a privilege to command them.

To Headquarters Base Camp to Siachen Glacier where I saw, learnt and experienced the cold heights of true Madness and feel qualified to talk of it.

To Late Col GS Gill, Vir Chakra my Directing Staff in the Academy, Brig HS Ghuman, Shaurya Chakra my first Commanding Officer and Col Inder Singh, my first Company Commander for daring me to be different.

To Brig MM Zaki, a highly evolved professional, from whom I learnt the nuances of harnessing the power of Madness.

To Col Satish P, Maj Gen PK Siwach, Col Sunil Prem, Wg Cdr Suhas Kelkar, IAF and Capt Rajvir Singh, IN, for their effort in scouring the forces grapevine and recommendations.

To all the Mad Vet Golden Oldies of my circle, who still continue to order me around like a youngster, thus ensuring I feel, live and stay young, and who have given their thumbs up for all my crazy and creative ideas, including this venture, and provided me grapevine inputs to put flesh on the bones.

To the profiled Mad Vets for consenting to share the saga of their entrepreneurship success and willingness to show the path to the oncoming waves of Mad Vets. For accepting the risk inherent in entrusting their brand image into the untested and unknown hands of a raw writer.

To Saroj, my wonderful life partner, who fully supported and inspired me in accomplishing the task at hand. She was more relieved than happy to see me contented in taking on a new (ad)venture, which confined me to the workstation rather than the outdoors.

To Arpana, my elder daughter, for undertaking creatives for the book and willingly taking on the nitty gritty of publication aspects. After going through my initial efforts, she commented I am sold to the theme.

To Kaveri, my younger daughter, for introducing me to the "21 days Abundance Challenge" of Deepak Chopra, which has made a world of difference to my creative skills.

To Saurabh, my elder son-in-law and trusted professional adviser, for providing incisive insights into the intricacies of commercial startup ventures and international corporate space.

To Rohan, my younger son-in-law, for initiating me into the exciting and wonderful world of high-altitude trekking. Unconcerned by the age factor, he took in stride my announcement of accompanying him on his forthcoming high-altitude trek. It is this attitude which motivates me to try new ideas every year.

To Atharv, my grandson, for not trashing my workstation despite carte blanche decree for freedom of action in the house granted to him by his grandmother. He does not yet comprehend the concept of ownership, so is happy to give away his prized toys and even happier to appropriate whatever catches his fancy for the moment.

To Tarun & Celia, for consenting to be my guides and initiating me into the psychic world of enormous beauty, extra-sensory perception and mysteries beyond the untrained mind.

To all my critics and fans for the brickbats and bouquets which this work shall beget, for having acknowledged my presence.

And last but not least to Zora & Sasha, my German Shepherds, for taking turns in keeping me company at my workstation on the cold nights, acting as my escort team during my early morning strolls in the forest to clear and energise my thoughts, and being my most loyal fans for whom I can do no wrong.

Abbreviations

. . . .

ACC	Army Cadet College
ADC	Aide – de - Camp
AI	Artificial Intelligence
AMD	Aircraft Manufacturing Depot
ASC	Army Service Corps
AQMG	Assistant Quarter Master General
BARC	Bhabha Atomic Research Centre
BDO	Block Development Officer
BRMD	Base Repair and Maintenance Depot
BRO	Border Roads Organisation
CBI	Central Bureau of Investigation
CO	Commanding Officer
CME	College of Military Engineering
COAS	Chief Of Army Staff
CPRS	Central Photo Reprocessing Section
DGP	Director General Police
Hrs	Hours
HAL	Hindustan Aeronautics Limited
HECL	Heavy Electricals Corporation Ltd
IA	Indian Army
IAF	Indian Air Force
IED	Improvised Explosive Device
IMA	Indian Military Academy
IN	Indian Navy

INS	Indian Naval Ship/Station
IPKF	Indian Peace Keeping Force
IPS	Indian Police Service
JCO	Junior Commissioned Officer
J&K	Jammu & Kashmir
JKLF	Jammu Kashmir Liberation Front
KAPP	Kalpakkam Atomic Power Project
LMC	Low Medical Category
Mad Vets	Mad Veterans
MH	Military Hospital
NCO	Non- Commissioned Officer
NDA	National Defence Academy
NIA	National Investigation Agency
NSG	National Security Guard
PABT	Pilot Aptitude Battery Test
PMO	Prime Minister Office
SAG	Special Action Group
SAM	Surface to Air Missile
SIT	Special Investigation Team
SSB	Services Selection Board
TADA	Terrorist And Disruptive Activities Act
VUCA	Volatile Uncertain Complex Ambiguous

Part I

Prologue

· ·

Never was there a time when I was not,
Nor thee, nor these lords of men;
Nor shall there ever be a time here after
When we all shall cease to be.

- Bhagwad Geeta (The Celestial Song)

The Story Is Born

. . . .

The urge to see beyond the horizon lies within and triggers the impulse to go still deeper within.

The Oxford dictionary defines **mad** as insane, frenzied, wildly foolish, wildly excited or infatuated, angry, wildly light hearted, with great energy or enthusiasm.

Crazy too is defined as insane or mad, foolish, extremely enthusiastic, made up of irregular pieces.

And then it struck me, almost forty plus years after happily leading my way of life of the mad breed of men.

You have to be crazy living atop a pile of kerosene-filled jerry cans, placed above ammunition stacks, at heights above 20,000 feet, braving unthinkable below-zero temperatures and freezing winds, for 3 to 4 months at a stretch, confined to an area of 50 square metres, with ten other crazy people breathing down your neck 24×7.

You have to be mad driving a 40 tonne tracked monster, in the dead of a pitched dark night, with all headlights off, over crazily undulating dunes, breathing in fine dust with every breath, every touch of your bare skin to the damned iron you are slogging on begetting blisters or peeled off skin depending on whether its midday or midnight, for 72 to 96 hours at a stretch.

You have to be creatively crazy to lay live mines in pitch darkness, over unknown terrain, each one of which could blow you to smithereens or worse still maim you for life. And even more crazy for following the reverse drill on the following night.

You have to be mad to raise toasts to the good health of your martyrs, comrades in arms, your sub-unit, your *Paltan* and your country till the wee hours of the morning and yet be on time for the early morning physical fitness parade, willingly taking on the young gazelles of your outfit to show who the boss is.

You have to be crazy to hear the sounds of arty shells and bullets flying fast and thick overhead and correctly guess those meant for you and those for the neighbours and take a walk accordingly.

You have to be mad to take off with all available aircraft on base, immediately after an air crash, without discerning the cause of accident.

You have to be crazy to live in cramped quarters in an armoured submersible for weeks and months at a stretch, hundreds of feet below the surface, sharing sleeping bunks, seeing neither the sun nor the stars, ensuring no sound escapes the submersible, wondering at the origin of the slightest of creaking sound, trying not to think of your fate if the engine fails or the hull seam develops a leak.

You have to be crazier still to put on the block your savings in a venture you know nothing about and succeed like mad beyond your wildest dreams.

But you understand that you are conventionally neither mad nor crazy when you have, for the umpteenth time, refused to be provoked by the "ignoramus" lout for gazing at you with that knowing and all too familiar smile, which makes it very, very clear of what he thinks of your intelligence, for wasting time in constructing a shaky bridge across a water obstacle, for hours at end, in hot sunshine, when you could just as easily cross over an existing bridge a mere hundred metres upstream.

All of this and more was going through my mind as I stepped into the forest for my morning walk duly accompanied by my escort team of Zora & Sasha, the German Shepherds. An early childhood memory, embedded deep in the subconscious mind, of listening to the Puranic tale of a Karma Yogi from my grandmother, suddenly flashed in my consciousness. It got me thinking as to how many of us Karma Yogi Mad

Vets have been able to successfully transfer our madness into the new life. That's how this book begins.

It is about ten Karma Yogi Mad Vets of the Indian Armed Forces, who have roaringly explored the uncharted terrain in the entrepreneurial world. The only loose criteria being that their venture be a startup with no prior expertise in the chosen field. Is there a method in their madness, the strategy they adopted, availability of a support structure, a common formula for success achieved or just that Karma Yogi Mad Vet sixth sense of a lifetime, which they earlier trusted their life with and were now willing to bet on commercially.

There is a source of madness deep within every human being which, if developed, leads to a highly evolved sixth sense of a Karma Yogi and an unquenchable thirst to accept risk and go beyond the conventional wisdom in searching new horizons, ideas, innovations and activities. It is this evolved sixth sense and unquenchable thirst which identifies the true blue Karma Yogi Mad Vet.

The book explores all of this and more.

* * *

Nine Realms of the Happy Veterans

. . . .

I wished for all things that I might enjoy life,
And was granted life that I might enjoy all things.

- Anonymous Soldier (on safe return)

It takes all kinds to make a world. There are personal likes and dislikes, varying thoughts and perceptions of a single situation, differing family and professional circumstances, dissimilar interests, attitudes and reactions, all of which play their role to make our world so beautiful, complex and unpredictable.

Bidding farewell to life with the armed forces can be both exhilarating and traumatic. It is a cutting off from one of the most comprehensive support systems. Unless planned well in advance, it could be a major source of misery and untold unhappiness.

To be happy and yet do nothing is an art and the most difficult to master. So it is essential to define to yourself ***what makes you happy*** prior to moving to the new stage of your life. Your devotion to duty needs to be transformed to your hobbies, your passions, adding richness and variety to your life. Broad realms of the 'established' post-retirement activities of the veterans are enumerated in the ensuing paragraphs. This brief is definitely not comprehensive, nor is there any attempt to establish any inter-se priority in the sequence of listing and is shared only to showcase the vitality and variety of the happiness quotient.

There are the Fault Finders, experts at finding faults in organisations, systems, equipment, personalities, nature, you name it. Unable to adjust to the chaos of life outside the army, cut off from the support system they have banked on all throughout their professional life, they revert to being critic and cynic par excellence. They *happily* immerse themselves in the tried and tested role, even at the cost of being distanced from their environment. Their value to their spouse and loved ones lies in being useful to put down plans, ideas and activities of near and dear ones they don't want implemented.

The Father Figures are *happily* domesticated and contented, showering love and attention on their grandchildren and following them for as long as health permits. They are contented and secure living the passion of the spouse.

The Social Elites are *happily* busy in golfing, clubbing and socialising as was their wont hithertofore. Financially secure, nothing has changed for them, not even the excuses to their spouse. Living the passion dear to self and the spouse, happiness is theirs to command.

The Corporate Warriors, the professionals and technicians, take up work in the corporate or social sector and immerse themselves in their new assignment. They have just changed the colour of their uniform and are *happily* busy in their new work profile, safe and secure as part of a new support system. Happiness is theirs, as there is no impact on the domestic domain of the spouse.

The Thinkers and Orators of the fraternity *happily* take to their role in strategic Think Tanks and as Motivational Speakers and defenders of The Faith in social and visual media like fish to water. The strategists and advisors work behind the semi-secretive veil of their profession as hithertofore movers and shakers par excellence. The motivational speakers and life skill coaches, endowed with oratory skills, which can charm a sparrow down the tree, use their rich experience to motivate the institutional and corporate 'youngs,' happily basking in the adulation of their audience in return. It takes time for the Social & Visual Media veterans to understand the nuances of 'TRP' and then they get going ready to bludgeon to submission, with their tongue, any opposition to The Faith. Happiness of the spouse too is ensured in reflective glory.

The Seekers and Spiritualists, freed from the strait jacket of army life, *happily* turn to seeking bliss, solace and wisdom by immersing themselves in search for higher meaning of life. They generally gravitate into the holy company of Seers, administering ashrams, delving into spiritual mysteries and experiencing true happiness. The rare among them attain the exalted stature of an evolved Guru.

The practitioners of the art of *happily* doing nothing are also known to exist but with indeterminate results as to longevity of their happiness, and are generally lone rangers.

The Ancestrals, lucky enough to inherit resources, tend to gravitate back to their roots, *happily* administering their inheritance, benignly impacting the quality of life in their surroundings and giving back to the environment from within their means.

Then there are the Path Finders, the Mad Vets who have *happily* carried forward their zest for life, fire in their bellies undimmed, passions still free flowing, capacity to accept risks still alive and thirst to explore more frontiers insatiable. Happiest among them are those who do not seek full external independence. They are the ones who have performed beyond the wildest dreams of their recruiters and who still answer the armed forces recruitment one liners in the affirmative - Do you have it in you! Live your passions! Dare to win! Realise your dreams! The entrepreneur sector is their new battlefield.

It is this last segment which is the cynosure of this narrative.

* * *

This poetry underlines what all this Passion, this Madness is about....

CALL TO ARMS A PASSION CALLED ARMY

Army, like priesthood, is a calling.
Either you have it, or you don't have it in you.
It is a calling closest to nature,
For does it not follow the three laws of nature.
Survival of the fittest, the Right of might, Inequality the way of life.
Everything else is Utopia.

While the business of business is making money,
We indulge in trading life.
It is not for the penny pushers
Nor the faint hearted.
You are in the wrong calling if you do not have it in you.

Screaming and kicking, you were not dragged in,
Eyes wide open, you volunteered to our way.
Do not corrupt with your penny dreams,
The call to arms is definitely not for you.
Honour our calling by returning to yours,
Go out and profess your penny-pushing ways.

The awe and wonder at the power to command,
To pulverise the enemy in mortal combat.
The flow of adrenalin while closing for the kill,
And wild exhilaration in the final charge.
The thrill of matching wits with an enemy devious,
To induce him to kill his own.

The indomitable spirit in taking on nature,
In its coldest fury and most awesome form.
The emotional high in diving to ground zero,
And the world you look down on.

The trepidation of stepping into Vikramaditya shoes,
The awesome responsibility that comes,
When you are the Judge, the Juror, Prosecutor and Executor all rolled
into one.
The determination to be ruthless when the task demands.
The trauma to sacrifice the dearest,
To save the other nine.
Honour the calling by standing Tall,
And with dignity you serve.

The courage of conviction, on the righteous path,
To take on the world.
In support of comrades lay everything on line.
The tremendous faith your subordinates feel,
As you enter the field when lost everything seems,
To snatch victory from certain defeat.

The loneliness you beget as the Leader's way,
The sweat you demand to ward off future loss of blood.
The glint of faith your subordinates reflect
Is payment enough which your presence begets
In the darkest of hours.
Oh what would you not do
To beget this payment, again and again.

The compassion towards the victims in times of strife,
The joy of saving lives from nature's fury,
The faith in the eyes of the distressed,
On seeing our Flag,
The smell of fear from the unholy, on hearing our treads.

The gentleness for the lady, always alongside you,
With a smile on her face, and tears hidden in the heart,
Bidding you to battle, again and again.
And the look in her eyes, when she welcomes you back.
The pride for the children when they stand up to the world,
To emulate your way and the principles you taught.

To witness the pristine sunrise of yet another day,
To admire the nature on a post far away.
To hear finality of life as 'Last Post' is sound,
And understanding rebirth in the 'Rouse.'
The dawning of realisation is finally yours,
Of the Almighty and his omnipotent ways,
When wishing for all things, so life you could enjoy,
And life itself being granted,
So things you could enjoy.

Our salute to the Calling, Oh so noble;
Hail the Almighty and the devil be damned.
Oh! What would I not give for a compact with Him,
For bringing me to this Calling,
Again and Again.

- Col RS Sidhu

* * *

Part II

The Ten Karma Yogi Mad Vets

When passion calls, barriers fall apart,
Pran surges the mind and the curtain is furled;
Stars are but stepping stones to the *Akash* that I command.

The Journey from Special Force to Special Director Cinematography

"Maj Ravi always dreams big, unrestrained by constraints of resources. He is born to be a Commando. Very tough, very sharp and has supreme confidence in his ability to deliver the goods."

- An Anonymous Black Cat

Three-and-a-half-year tenure with the elite NSG, leading special operations against terrorist organisations in J&K, Punjab and with IPKF in Sri Lanka, winner of Sena Medal for Gallantry, twice winner of Chief of Army Staff Commendation Card for Distinguished Service, Winner of Director General of National Security Guards Commendation Card for exemplary services, participant in high profile special operations against killers of former Indian Prime Minister Shri Rajiv Gandhi.

Director, story writer, screenplay writer, dialogue writer and actor in the Malayalam film industry, credited with directing ten and working in more than two dozen films, privileged to work with film industry top names such as film makers Priyadarshan, Rajkumar Santoshi, Kamal Haasan and Mani Ratnam, directing Malayalam film superstars such as Mohanlal, Mammooty and Prithvi Raj and winner of **Kerala State**

Award in 2006 for Best Screenplay Award for *Keerthi Chakra*, **Asianet Film Awards** in 2006 for Best Director Award for *Keerthi Chakra*, Special Honour Jury Award in 2008 for *Kurukshetra*, Best Feature Film on National Integration Award in 2010 for *Kandahar*.

AK Ravindran, aka Ravi, is the proverbial destiny's child. His life's journey reveals two very strong strands in his mental makeup. His unshakeable belief in destiny and his willingness to go to any extreme to get what catches his fancy. The root cause of his first major sorrow can be traced to this second strand.

Studying in a school in Koottanad village in District Palakkad of Kerala, Ravi was in 9th standard when he took a fancy to a girl studying in standard 8. So Ravi failed in his 9th standard school exams. Ravi and his fancy were now in the same class. However, the orthodox social mores of the 70s ensured that Ravi could not get an opportunity to even converse with the classmate, he so fancied, through the year. It was only when they got promoted to 10th standard that he got an opportunity to engage with her in conversation. Then destiny intervened. Ravi's first romantic note upset her enough to vehemently convey her displeasure, leading to a fallout between them. She cleared her 10th board exams, and Ravi failed.

Ravi was the elder of two siblings and was born in Pattambi, District Palakkad in Kerala, in June 1958. His father, an ASC veteran of Second World War, had served in Burma and Baluchistan. A strict disciplinarian, he ruled his family with an iron hand. The family earnings were low, and the initial years were a struggle. The shenanigans of Ravi as well as his being the perennial rebel of the family became a sore point with his extended family of uncles and aunts. But time changes perceptions, and today he is the most successful of the entire family, and their viewpoints too have changed.

As a tenth standard dropout, Ravi saw a bleak future staring at him. One fine day, he decided to leave home unannounced, to seek better opportunities in Bombay, now Mumbai. On reaching Bombay, Ravi proceeded to meet his maternal uncle, a retired Commodore from the

IN and ex Commandant of INS Kunjali. The Commodore promptly threw him out of the house on getting to know the circumstances of his arrival in Bombay.

Ravi spent the next three days on a platform at Bombay VT railway station, surviving only on bananas, till his money ran out. To while away his time, he looked at advertisements adorning the billboards. One of the posters displayed was of the movie *Sholay*. Something in the portrait of Amitabh Bachchan, one of the leading stars of the movie, held his attention. He felt drawn towards Amitabh Bachchan and daydreamed of being in his company. Unknown to him then, it would take a quarter of a century for the innocent dream of a runaway from home to meet the megastar of Bollywood to materialise.

By now tired and hungry, while rummaging through his meagre belongings, he came across an old notebook of his father, which he had brought with him. While thumbing through the notebook, he came across the particulars of a distant relative who was running a hotel in Koliwada locality. It was midnight by the time Ravi reached the hotel of his relative. Ravi's response to all queries was that he was hungry. Says Ravi, "First time in my life I realised what hunger pain is. Such was the impact that even to this day I go out of my way to feed any hungry person I come across, irrespective of cost."

Within a month, Ravi got a message from his uncle, who was a combatant clerk with 253 Medium Regiment of Artillery at Babina, near Jhansi in Uttar Pradesh, to appear for an existing vacancy of Wireless Operator, in Unit Headquarter Enrolment Quota. Ravi rushed to Babina, appeared for the exam and passed with flying colours.

Life as a Soldier

On 31 January 1976, Ravi reported at Corps of Artillery Centre, Nasik in Maharashtra for recruit training. By the third day, Ravi was facing Court Martial proceedings. The tough training regimen of a recruit made Ravi perpetually hungry, and he would run at meal times to the Langar so that he could be first in the queue for meals. The Langar Commander, a Naik, took instant dislike to Ravi, and on a flimsy excuse used foul language, casting racial aspersion, and also physically manhandled him. Ravi, more injured by the racial slur than the physical manhandling, retaliated and injured the Langar Commander. Ravi followed up by getting twelve fellow recruits to sign a joint petition to the CO against the actions of the Langar Commander. In the words of Ravi, "How was I to know that joint petition is a more seriously viewed act than physical abuse? So, dressed in loose khaki shorts hanging below the knees, with a rope tied in lieu of belt and loose khaki shirt, looking every bit like Oliver Twist, I found myself standing in the CO's Orderly Room. On looking up I saw behind the CO's desk a board displaying names of all COs. There I was surprised to see the last name as Lt Col TMS Nair, an uncle of mine, and I blurted out the fact unwittingly. The CO was surprised, but it was enough to get a patient hearing. It enabled me to put across our side of the story in broken Hindi, learnt in my short stay at Bombay, and broken English learnt in school. The thirteen of us were absolved, and the Langar Commander ended up being reduced to ranks from Naik." Destiny had intervened.

Recruit Squad 872, to which Ravi belonged, became the target of NCO instructors for showing temerity of reporting against a fellow NCO. Life became hell, but it also ensured that 872 became the toughest squad in the Artillery Centre. Shortly thereafter, trials for Athletics Team were held, and Ravi was selected to represent the Battery Team in the 800-metre run. During practice, Ravi took a chance at attempting Pole Vault successfully. His talent for Pole Vault was noticed, and he got selected for the Centre Athletics team in Pole Vault. As a proud member of the Centre Athletics team, he switched from the regulation Khakis, of a recruit, to Whites. He was now beyond the reach of the vindictive NCOs. In the next six months, he went on to represent the Artillery Centre in Pole Vault at the Services Athletics Meet.

On successful completion of his recruit training, Ravi was posted to 40 Medium Regiment of Artillery. His dedication and competence was noted, and soon he was nominated as the Wireless Operator of the CO.

Unfortunately, he met with an accident while returning by train from collective training in Rajasthan and ended up with two broken ribs. He was placed in temporary LMC. Capt FU Ahmed, popularly known as Fussy Ahmed, in his unit, had developed a liking for Ravi, drawn by his simplicity, commitment and straightforwardness. Fussy Ahmed got Ravi detailed to attend Army Higher Secondary Examination during his period of LMC. Ravi studied hard and cleared his examinations. He was now eligible to appear for ACC examinations for entry into Commissioned Officers cadre. On being declared physically fit, Ravi represented his unit in formation athletics championship in Pole Vault and was promoted as Unpaid Lance Naik.

Ravi now earnestly began preparing for ACC exams, under the guidance of Fussy Ahmed. Some of the JCOs of the unit took umbrage at Ravi's attempt to upgrade himself to above their status. In the unit 2200 hrs is lights out time. A day before the exams, while studying under a streetlight, he was accosted for not observing anti-malaria precautions by the Regiment Subedar Major and another JCO from the Regiment Headquarter, returning from the JCO Mess. A verbal altercation followed, and the Regiment Headquarter JCO slapped Ravi, who retaliated. This resulted in Ravi being placed under arrest for assault and affray. Ravi saw his chance to appear for ACC exams evaporate. It was Fussy Ahmed's intervention on his behalf, with the CO, which saved the day for Ravi. He got a temporary reprieve, enabling him to appear in the ACC exam. The very next day, Ravi was demoted to Sepoy and sentenced to 28 days imprisonment in Quarter Guard. This merited a 'red ink' entry in the dossier of Ravi, a severe demerit, which could ruin his chance to be an officer. The JCOs were smug at extinguishing the dreams of an 'upstart' Other Rank. Much later, an anguished Ravi privately accosted the JCO responsible for stage managing the incident and pledged to become an officer and return to the unit, just for the pleasure to be saluted by the JCO.

In the army, the adage "Everything is fair in war and love" is taken very seriously. Just add peace time sports competition to the adage, for they are contested equally fiercely. Fortunately for Ravi, the formation athletics championship was due in a few days. Being a star athlete, his sentence was commuted. Ravi won his Pole Vault event and in appreciation regained his rank of Unpaid Lance Naik. Destiny had again intervened in his favour.

Soon he got a call to appear for SSB interview at Bangalore. It was a close call. The issue of 'red ink' entry in the dossier was broached during the interview. Fortunately for him, his frank narrative of the incident carried the day. Ravi could not resist tempting fate even under such trying circumstances. In the words of Ravi, "During the final day President's interview, with full board in attendance, I was asked about my previous night's escapade. I truthfully replied that I had come from field area and had heard about Bangalore's night life. Hence, on my last night in the station, I bunked to witness a cabaret show. Since it was late night and the main gate of the SSB Selection Centre campus was closed, I tried bribing the guard on duty to let me in. The guard refused to be tempted by the offered bribe. I then jumped over the wall and entered. Even if I fail the interview, I will have the satisfaction of at least one achievement."

Only two aspirants were selected, Ravi and another candidate Javed Husain. Destiny had again stood by Ravi. He joined ACC Wing at IMA, Dehradun in 1980 for three years pre-commission training. Javed and Ravi became the best of friends. An unfortunate incident resulted in Ravi being relegated by one term. To pep up Ravi, Javed welcomed him with sweets and aerated soft drinks. Javed was now senior to Ravi. The boot was on the other foot when a few days before the Passing Out Parade, Javed also got relegated. It was now Ravi's turn to pep up Javed with sweets and aerated soft drinks. Both the friends were once again course mates. In the final term, Ravi was awarded the coveted appointment of Wing Cadet Adjutant, a fitting tribute to his professional competence. Keeping in mind the pledge made to his unit JCO, Ravi opted for Artillery. It is rare indeed for an ACC Gentleman Cadet to be given commission into the Arm/Service where he has served in the ranks. But Ravi was high in the order of merit to be given his choice and was commissioned into 262 Medium Regiment of Artillery in 1984. His friend Javed was commissioned into ASC.

Life as an Officer

Says Ravi, "My first action as an officer was to visit 40 Medium Regiment to personally express my thanks to Fussy Ahmed and his wife, who was like a mother to me. Without their efforts to look after my interest I would not have become an officer. Fussy Ahmed is now happily retired and settled in Lucknow, but even today I am in touch with him. Somewhere at the back of my mind was also my pride to redeem my pledge to be saluted by the JCO who had conspired against me."

It was 1987 and Ravi, as member of The Services athletics team, was temporarily attached to an army unit in Delhi to enable him to try out and practice with the newly introduced Pole Vault fibre glass pole in the National Stadium at Delhi. During a practice session, he was noticed by Ved Marwah, the then Director General, NSG, the elite special force of the country. Within a short period, Ravi got a call to attend probation training for induction into the NSG. Officers with at least five to six years' service are generally selected for deputation with the NSG. Ravi had barely three years' service as an officer, a rare distinction.

NSG probation is gruelling, involving battle physical efficiency tests, battle assault obstacle course, combat weapon firing, counter terrorist operations training, karate and skill development among other technical and specialised training. Ravi topped all the tests and the course. By dint of sheer hard work and merit, he had risen from the ranks and gained entry as an officer into the hallowed portals of an elite Special Force. In early 1988, he was assigned 51 SAG in the NSG. Special operations were ongoing in J&K, Punjab and North East India, and in support of IPKF operations in Sri Lanka. For Ravi, there would be ample opportunities for excitement and demonstrating battlefield leadership.

In December 1988 Ravi got married to Anita, and in January 1989 he was deployed on his first special mission, to free Rubaiya Sayeed who had been kidnapped by terrorists in J&K. She also happened to be the daughter of Mufti Mohammad Sayeed, the then Home Minister of India. The operation was called off at the last minute despite the target being sighted. Four jailed terrorists of JKLF were freed in return for securing the release of Rubaiya Sayeed. These terrorists subsequently went on to hijack the Indian Airlines flight IC – 814 to Kandahar in Afghanistan.

Ravi's first big success was a counter militancy operation in 1989. Intelligence inputs had revealed six militants holed up in a farmhouse amongst *chari,* tall, green cattle fodder fields. Guided by local police, Ravi's team reached the hideout around 0900 hrs. The militants had already shot two central police personnel who had attempted to approach the hideout, and their dead bodies were visible in an open field. The suspected farmhouse lay in the midst of the *chari* fields. By now the militants had slipped out from the farmhouse to hide in the *chari* fields, of approximately football field size, where visibility was zero.

The militants started firing their weapons on the security forces deployed in outer cordon. Ravi zeroed in on their location by identifying the smoke puffs emanating from their weapons and fired airburst rockets on the identified location. The quantum of fire from the terrorists decreased, indicating casualties suffered by them. The operation was being conducted in close proximity to the International Border, and the thick and high crops provided ideal cover to escape in poor visibility hours. Hence there was urgency to finish the operation before daylight was over. Ravi then requisitioned a cross-country mobility vehicle modified as an armoured half truck. Ravi led an assault team, mounted on the modified vehicle, to close in for the kill. The driver of the vehicle received a gunshot injury on his arm.

In the ensuing close quarter battle, six militants were killed. While undertaking search operations, the assault team heard rustling in the undergrowth. It was the quick reflexes of the Special Forces which saved the day. There was a seventh militant as well. He too was shot dead before he could do any harm. Ravi learnt the vital lesson of confirming and reconfirming reliability of information before launching special operations. It was late afternoon by the time the operation was successfully completed. Ravi and Capt RR Patel, Regimental Medical Officer of the unit and a highly proficient commando, were awarded Sena Medal for gallantry for the operation. Three Other Ranks, who also participated in the same operation, were awarded with Chief of Army Staff Commendation Card for gallantry. Ravi had established his credentials under fire.

Ravi, with his team, was an active participant in several anti-militancy operations in J&K and Punjab. While deployed with his team in support of Punjab Police for counter-insurgency operations, Ravi came in close contact with Mr KPS Gill, the then DGP, Punjab. In Ravi's words, "Mr KPS Gill was one of the most dedicated and professional police officers I have met. He was tough as nails, never smiled, and his face always wore a disconcerting deadpan, even stony, look. During a span of four days, our team had conducted three successful special operations with his knowledge. Suddenly, I was called back to Delhi by my CO. It was highly disappointing for me. I spent the next two weeks in debriefing about the operations. Then abruptly, I was ordered to move back to Punjab to join our Team. I found it most perplexing. Even my query about the sudden recall and return did not elicit any response from my CO. On reaching Amritsar, I directly proceeded to Punjab Police Headquarters for meeting with the DGP. On a hunch, I asked him about my sudden move out and return to operational duty with him. The DGP just clasped my shoulders and pressed me to sit in the chair. After seating himself, he responded saying 'You were sent back to Delhi to cool down because success closes eyes.' I was deeply touched by his care for his team, though he never showed it."

"In another incident, we had just conducted a very successful operation, and the DGP reached the site. While seeing him off, I lightly commented that he had not complimented our team for the wonderful success. 'I don't want to stop you with a pat on the back; I expect more from you' was his crisp response," Ravi emotionally recalls.

On 25 January 1990, J&K militants had killed four IAF personnel and injured several others in a terrorist attack. Yasin Malik and his JKLF group were believed to be the alleged perpetrators. Ravi led the NSG operations wherein four militants responsible for the attack were captured alive in a pre-dawn raid in their hideout. Yasin Malik is now facing trial in a TADA Court for the offence.

In May 1991, Late Shri Rajiv Gandhi, the ex-Prime Minister of India was assassinated, leading to one of the most intense investigations to apprehend his killers. Mr DR Karthikeyan was appointed as head of SIT of CBI to investigate the assassination and arrest the culprits. Ravi was part of the NSG team placed in support of the SIT for conducting operations to arrest the culprits as and when identified and located. The Team was placed under Deputy Inspector General of Police Radha Vinod Raju, the operations and investigation head of the SIT. The task for the NSG Team was to apprehend the culprits alive and prevent them from committing suicide by consuming cyanide.

Ravi shares, "Mr Radha Vinod Raju was one of the most professional, patriotic and dedicated IPS officers. Not once did he give indication that his wife was a cancer patient and bed ridden while being in discreet touch over phone to monitor her progress. He went on to become the first Director of NIA and himself also died from cancer two years after his retirement. On 02 August 1991, information was received of the suspects being holed up in a house in Indira Nagar locality of Bangalore. Our team was launched in broad daylight, and we blasted our way into the hideout. Two suspects, hiding inside, consumed cyanide in attempted suicide. The accompanying medicos, equipped for this contingency, were able to revive one by administering an antidote; the second suspect died. Unfortunately, the main accused, Sivarasan, had already escaped from the same house a night before."

Ravi continues, "Then on 18 August, Sivarasan and his accomplices were identified to be hiding in a house in Konanakunte area in Jayanagar,

Karnataka. It was a busy residential area. An outer cordon was unobtrusively deployed, and we moved into position for assault by 2200 hrs. However, to our surprise, Mr DR Karthikeyan issued instructions that no action will be taken till he reaches the site to personally supervise the operation. He reached the site only by 19 August evening. We had to wait the whole night and most of the next day. The interim period was used to mount surveillance on the target by establishing lookouts disguised as mango sellers and auto-rickshaw drivers. But the time lag was too long, and the public in the vicinity sensed something amiss. Soon a crowd gathered in the area. The surprise element had been lost. On reaching the site Mr DR Karthikeyan asked to be briefed on the operational plan. Execution of special operations is our forte, and here was a senior officer, who had inordinately delayed the execution of a nationally sensitive operation by wanting to interfere beyond his field of expertise. I was naturally frustrated and responded that our plan got over once he had asked us to wait for his arrival and now we would go as per his plan. I then walked back to the target area which was 400 metres away and positioned myself behind a stationary vehicle. Within minutes weapon shots were fired onto us from within the target house. One of our team was injured by gunshot but luckily survived. On 20 August at 0500 hrs we were finally given the go ahead. When we forced entry, to our chagrin, we found all suspects inside had by then died by consuming cyanide. Seven dead bodies were recovered, including that of Sivarasan, who had committed suicide by shooting himself. An opportunity for successful accomplishment of mission had been sacrificed at the altar of ego."

In special operations speed of decision and dexterity of execution are critical for success. Almost thirty years later while recalling the incident, Ravi's exasperation still comes out clearly, where success was theirs for the taking but for the delay in getting the crucial green signal to launch the operation. Ravi is still unable to accept certain inconsistencies in the events following the assassination and the actions of the SIT and is categorical in saying, "Even thirty years later, this failure rankles, for failure it was, as we were tasked to capture the suspects alive. At times I stay awake in the night thinking about plausible reasons to delay the launch of operation by 36 hours, and I still can't think of any. I do not believe in the conspiracy theories, but the assassination of an ex-Prime Minister is a highly emotive issue and of great national import, necessitating laying to rest the bogeys and conspiracy theories surrounding it. The appropriate authorities owe it to the nation to lead an investigation to uncover the facts of the thirty-six hour delay in orders to launch the operation; Mr Karthikeyan's presence in Hyderabad, the then place of residence of his family, on 18 August 1991 a Sunday, rather than at the spot of the most critical juncture of his mandate; strangeness of only the ex-Prime Minister, the police personnel and innocent public dying in the blast at a political rally and all other political personalities remaining unscathed; and lastly the fact of SIT during the course of investigation avoiding questioning political figures present at the rally ground."

Ravi also served on special assignment in support of IPKF in Sri Lanka, but with the decision for deinduction of the Force from the island he rejoined his Team at Gurgaon.

When queried about his feelings on his tenure with 51 SAG, Ravi said, "Even today my belief is firm that destiny and death come to you only when fated. I had volunteered for NSG to feel the high of being in the thick of action. Even when not on operations, we were continuously on our toes, because the CO would test us at odd hours without notice. More than the honours and awards it begot me, what I rate as my biggest achievement with NSG is that there were no fatal casualties of my colleagues and subordinates during these three and a half years of almost never-ending special operations. I also had developed a 'singing' relationship with my CO, who retired as a Major General while I came out as a Major. Even today we keep in regular touch and share our joys and sorrows."

On completion of his tenure with the NSG, in December 1991, Ravi was posted as ADC (Security) to Gen SF Rodrigues, COAS. Ravi held this appointment till August 1993, resulting in absence of six years from his parent Regiment. His knowledge of Artillery had become rusted. So he applied for a transfer to the Intelligence Corps which was accepted, and he was posted to an Intelligence unit deployed at Leh. In July 1996, he prepared his first detailed report, based on human intelligence inputs, on enhanced Pakistan Army activities in POK. His intelligence analysis did not find favour within his hierarchy, and the report was buried in files. This impacted him deeply enough to apply for premature release from the army. His resignation was accepted, and he left the army the same year, in 1996. Kargil conflict in 1999 served to vindicate his intelligence stand. But it was of small satisfaction; Maj AK Ravindran, aka Ravi, had already shed his Olive Greens.

The Black Cats are a very exclusive and well-knit community which lives by their own code of conduct. Unwillingness to talk about their operations and colleagues is inbuilt into their psyche. But when kindred spirits interact, tongues loosen. When coaxed to talk about Ravindran, in strictest of confidence, the general consensus is that he was born to be a commando, very tough, very sharp and with supreme confidence in his ability to deliver the goods. One of his erstwhile colleagues went on to add that he always dreamt big, unfettered by the constraints of resources at hand.

Changing the Uniform

When he left the army in 1998, Major Ravi had two strands dominating his thoughts. One was confidence in his own ability to succeed in whatever venture he would decide to pick up. The second was to work for himself and not under anyone else. Post release from the army, he would often spend his spare time, and it was in abundance, with his friends Mohanlal and Priyadarshan.

When queried about the origins of his friendship with the duo, Ravi was diffident. "Mohanlal and Priyadarshan had come to Port Blair, Andaman Islands, for the shooting of their film *Kalapani* while I was posted there. Someone apprised Mohanlal that one of the commandos involved in the hunt for killers of Late Shri Rajiv Gandhi was also in the station. He then expressed a desire to meet me and sent a note to this effect. That was the start of our friendship," said Ravi.

Initially, Ravi would get some commercial acts, which would pay him up to two thousand rupees for a day's work. His first major break came in the year 2000, when he got a call from Rajkumar Santoshi to assist him with the realistic portrayal of matters pertaining to army in his film *Pukar*. Cinematographer-director Santosh Sivan was the one who had recommended Ravi for the assignment. While working on the sets of *Pukar* for the next three years, Ravi felt drawn towards the role of a director in movies. His work as a military consultant in films gave him adequate learning opportunities while working in close consultation with several reputed directors.

Directorial Innings

After acting in several Malayalam films, Ravi began to focus more on the role of a director. He made his directorial debut as independent director in 2006, with *Keerthi Chakra*, a film on Kashmir militancy, starring Mohanlal. He wrote his own story, based on the special operation wherein he was awarded for gallantry and approached Mohanlal for accepting the lead role. The film proved to be a big hit at the box office and also won him the Kerala State Award for Best Screenplay.

In 2007, he directed *Mission 90 Days*, based on the Rajiv Gandhi assassination case, starring Mammooty. He was also the writer and an actor in the film.

His third project *Kurukshetra*, based on the Kargil War and starring Mohanlal, was a sequel to *Keerthi Chakra*. Ravi was both the director and writer of the film.

The 2010 film *Kandahar,* starring Mohanlal, was a third instalment to the Major Mahadevan film series. Ravi featured in the film as director, writer and actor.

In 2012, he directed *Karma Yodha* starring Mohanlal. Ravi was the film's co-producer, director and writer.

He was the director and writer for *Picket 43*, starring Prithviraj and Javed Jaffrey. The film released in 2015 and turned out to be a hit.

1971 Beyond Borders, starring Mohanlal, released in 2017, was Ravi's fourth film in the Major Mahadevan series. He was the director and writer of the film.

Maj Ravi has a long string of successful movies in his bag, and is an accomplished director, actor, screenplay, story and dialogue writer. He is now heading towards the next instalment in the Major Mahadevan series. In this film, says Ravi, "The focus is on individuals rather than the war and will portray the relationships that are forged during the war."

On the realisation of his dreams, he says, "My success in the film industry revived my memory of the runaway brat and daydreams to be with Amitji. The day came when after due appointment, I approached him for accepting a role in my next film *Kandahar*. Amitji listened attentively to the proposed role play and graciously gave his consent. That day I realised that if you dream sincerely, they do come true."

"I spent three days in the company of that great show personality in Ooty while shooting for his role play in the film. He refused to accept any remuneration for his act, saying in a matter of fact way, that he got extreme pleasure in portraying the assigned character role and would not take any remuneration for it. The preview of the film was held at Leela Kempinsky Hotel, duly attended by Amitji. There I narrated my dream and its realisation in front of the whole audience and touched his feet humbly," recalls Maj Ravi.

Dada Saheb Phalke Award is India's highest National Award in Cinema. The recipient is selected by a committee consisting of eminent personalities from the Indian film industry. Shri Amitabh Bachhan was selected for the National Dada Saheb Phalke Award for 2018. In an interesting aside, Maj Ravi was one of the members of the selection committee.

Asked to talk about the work ethics of the film industry, Ravi says, "As an army man when I joined the film industry, I was used to a disciplined way of life. Right from our academy days during training, the value of discipline in life is drilled into us. We understand the value of life, value for time and value for money. By the time we come out from the army and hang our uniform, this discipline has already become an integral part of our life. While making a film, I am guided by this aspect of discipline. It is like commanding a company of 150 men with different temperaments and different hierarchical positions, from a hero to the spot boy who serves tea. But the action has to unfold the way I, as a director, have conceived it to be. So if I have planned that the shooting will take place in minus twenty-five degrees Celsius at 0700 hrs tomorrow, then I must be at the spot at 0655 hrs. That's how we are taught in the army. The lead actor may be more valuable for the commercial success of the movie, but when the Captain is present before time, the others automatically follow the lead. The star cast may be late on one odd day, but then they will be on time, because they know that I will be on time and they don't have to waste time in waiting. Though some lead personalities are known to throw tantrums, I have not faced any such situation. Leading by personal example does make a difference."

He continues, "So what happens. We save on time, which converts to saving on lots of money. Delay would lead to extension of shoot, and every additional day implies cost overruns. I have a record of completing all my film shoots within 30 days. Only my last film was done in 34 odd days. I shot the film *Picket 43* in Shopian, with Javed Jaffrey and Prithviraj, for ten days in minus twenty-five degrees Celsius temperature in four feet snow, ten days without snow and 2 more days in the village. So when others take 100 days for completing the shoot I am aghast at the cost burden that they would be adding and all because they lack discipline to adhere to the time schedule. A twelve-hour shoot from 0700 hrs in the morning to around 1900 hrs in the evening is good enough to give you 4 to 6 minutes of movie footage. So for a two-hour film, 20 to 25 days shoot is good enough. Thus, discipline has enabled me to control my production costs."

On his directorial style Ravi says, "When I do an army theme film I know what is feasible and what is not possible. I will never let the nation and the army down in my films, and I do not employ melodramatic dialogues. I let the actions of our soldiers speak for themselves. The way I picturise those action scenes is enough to raise patriotic fervour amongst the audience. My movie *Kargil* is a fine example of my style. When the victory is achieved on the icy heights of Kargil and ceasefire is announced, the hero of my film, a young Colonel, passionately declares his resolve to not move back one inch from the areas he has fought hard and won at the cost of precious lives of his men. I then use a voiceover of our then Prime Minister Shri Atal Vajpayee speaking in the vernacular, 'Colonel, wherever you are standing, plant the Indian flag there, turn around and say *Jai Hind*, this is now the territory of India.' The emotional impact of this dialogue was enough to raise the passions amongst the audience to stand on their seats and shout *'Bharat Mata ki Jai!'* and this includes Christians, Muslims, Hindus, Marxists and Congress and BJP supporters alike. At that moment of time I succeeded in getting all of them to forget their differences and stand united as Indians. This is the way I make the films. This is the advantage I have over the others in the industry, because I am an army man."

RAVI SPEAKS

Learnings from the Army

I joined the army at the age of seventeen plus years as a raw hand. Some of the basics of army discipline had already been taught to me by my father, a World War II soldier. He had his own way of instilling in me discipline, the value of time, sincerity and loyalty. That made it much easier for me to adjust to the army way of life. It has taught me to value and respect time and personal discipline. I get called to numerous social functions, and I am always on time. On a few occasions I find that while I have come at the appointed hour,

the function will take at least another couple of hours to commence. On one occasion I drove 180 km to attend a function. On reaching the spot I was surprised to find that the administrative arrangement would take at least another few hours to be completed. I waited for ten minutes and just drove back.

Whatever I am today is because of what I have learnt in the army. It has taught me empathy, focus on goals and faith in own capabilities.

Philosophy Towards Life

I lead an uprighteous life and practice what I preach. 'Let me live and I will not trouble' you has been my philosophy.

Personal Qualities that Have Helped You

Self-discipline, punctuality and my passion for work are the personal qualities which have held me in good stead. I just go ahead and do whatever is required to be done. My father and even my mother would always guide me to be sincere and dedicated to whatever task has been undertaken and not to look back to see if I am being watched.

Difficulties

In the cinema world, my biggest difficulties have materialised from people who do not respect time, and I have judiciously employed my experience of command in the army to overcome them. The army has taught me to lead from the front, which leads to developing an aura around my personality. This aura or power of personality has helped me in my difficult situations.

Impacting Life of Others

I have believed and followed Napoleon's dictum that you have only one life and death comes only once. So don't let the fear of death overcome the life you wish to lead. Death has an appointed time, and you cannot die before it. I never felt the fear of death. My boys developed this attitude and just concentrated on the task at hand. This enabled them to focus their entire energy on the operations and ensured that they did not get killed by their negligence.

Three Major Achievements

I had the initial 'go' to join the army as a soldier. But I didn't stop there and wanted to become an Officer so I could have the opportunity to lead and make decisions rather than be driven by what hierarchy had determined for me. Thus, I became an Officer. Now I could do something for the Nation the way I wanted it to be done. Then I wanted to join the NSG to be a commando and effectively undertake dangerous tasks in defence of my country. So I became a commando, topped the training and participated in numerous operations. The award of Sena Medal did not excite me as much as the fact that there have been no fatal casualties amongst my men in special operations under my command. This is my biggest achievement.

Next is the connect which I have been able to establish with my audience in the film industry.

Retaining my values and ethics is also one of my biggest achievements.

Advice for the Mad Vets

Do not measure success in materialistic terms. The impact of your work on the environment should be the measure of your success rather than the monetary gains.

Options for the Mad Vets to Undertake New Ventures

My advice is very simple: do what you are passionate about. Success will follow.

The Future of India

The biggest millstone around the country's neck is the politicians. We require more and more young, educated and patriotic citizens to join the political world. The public needs to be aware of the shenanigans of the politicians who divide us on every possible line, be it religious, social, regional, lingual, et al. At the end of the day, they sit together and protect each other's interests while we are kept mired in misery and hatred for each other. This is now changing for the better.

India is a country of dynamic young citizens, with strong family ties, multicultural ethos and innovative skills, an unbeatable combination. We are fighters. The Indian diaspora spread across the world too has added tremendously to the soft power enjoyed by us today in the world's financial and diplomatic centres.

This is India's century. We have a bright future to look forward to.

One Mantra for the Mad Vets
Carry forward your army values into your new profession.

Willingness to Mentor Mad Vets
But of course yes.

On the Role of Spouse
Anita is the strongest pillar of my life. When I decided to leave the army, she fully supported my decision. She has the responsibility of running the household, raising the children and managing our vast circle of relatives and family friends. This has left me free to concentrate on my profession with full dedication.

Half the things I don't tell her, for her own peace of mind. When she joined me and the army as a newly wedded wife, I was with the NSG. I could not share the details of my movements with her, and she did not know when she would see me next. Right since the beginning she has accepted the fact of my professional and personal life being two different compartments.

The fact that she does not interfere in my professional life is by itself one of the biggest supports for me.

* * *

Electrical & Solar Grid System Projects and Consultants

. . . .

I look forward to leaving this world while still at work, on my own two feet.

- Sgt Bhaurao Saraswat

Saraswat Engineering Services

Leading Aircraftman Bhaurao Saraswat was unaware that he was about to encounter the most defining moment of his life while attending the Services Selection Board interview, at Dehradun in 1963, for Commission as Pilot in the IAF. He cleared his interview and proceeded for his medical examination but got rejected for his leg length being half an inch less than the prescribed physical standards. That lack of half inch put paid to his dream to pilot aircrafts. Destiny would later go on to provide him solace to do the next best thing – five years of simulated flying while training the 'God's Own' fighter pilots of the IAF and be the best and youngest Sergeant Electrician of IAF in his time. His selection to the highly secretive special unit CPRS, directly attached to IAF Headquarters at Delhi, assignment on electrical checks for maiden flights of first three Avro aircraft manufactured at AMD at Kanpur, distinction of being 'Best in Trade' and 'Best Overall' in all technical courses attended by him, and later selection for training in USSR on the latest aircraft simulators are ample indicators of his being the best in his trade.

Set up in 1984 by Bhaurao Saraswat after shedding his uniform, Saraswat Engineering Services is today an INR 12 Crore annual turnover company with more than 100 employees on its direct rolls, is a registered vendor with Airports Authority of India, Mazagaon Docks, Nuclear Corporation of India, Indian Space Research Organisation and Hindustan Petroleum Corporation Ltd. among others and has executed all electrical works for:

> Design, supply, installation and commissioning of electrical equipment for Juhel Pharmaceutical plant in Nigeria in 2009-10
> Arcelor Mittal Railway Yard project for coal mines in Liberia in 2010-11
> Electrical work for multiple solar projects across India totalling more than 100 MW
> Electrical work at multiple airports across India including Mumbai, Nagpur, Guwahati, Goa, Vishakhapatnam, Trivandrum and Allahabad (under Tata Projects)

One can never underestimate the power of communication, especially in the people's tongue. Languages came naturally to Bhaurao. He could catch on a tongue effortlessly and speak like a native, a gift not many are blessed with. His fluency in English, Hindi, Marathi, Bengali, Punjabi and Russian gave Bhaurao an added advantage over his competitors in the entrepreneur world of multicultural Bombay.

Early Life

Bhaurao Saraswat was born in the village Wani, District Amravati in Maharashtra and was the eldest of five siblings. His father was a small farmer, and mother was a homemaker. Bhaurao completed his early schooling at the village primary school. Thereafter, his school education was a struggle, moving from one village to another, staying with relatives and friends, involving a daily hike of 4-5 km one way, and at times having to cross rivulets. He was brilliant in studies and would secure first/second position in class merit. In his Matriculation Board exams, Bhaurao secured above 70% marks, with distinction in four out of five subjects, and also had highest marks amongst all the seven schools of the region. His family could not finance his higher education, they being limited by resources and also motivation to pursue higher studies. Bhaurao was, however, determined and left no stone unturned to study further. Fortunately for Bhaurao, his school Managing Body came forward to assist him in securing admission in the engineering stream in a pre-university college. Even today, Bhaurao is grateful for those fortunes that came his way.

Life With IAF

After completing his pre-university and pre-professional engineering education, Bhaurao applied for enrolment into the IAF at a selection centre at Pulgaon, Maharashtra, and successfully qualified in the exams. In July 1960, he joined the IAF and was allotted electrical trade. After initial basic training, he was transferred to Air Force Technical Training College – later redesignated as School – at Kanpur in Uttar Pradesh. He was a keen learner and performed well in the weekly exams. He has maintained his inquisitive attitude even today and can often be found watching *HOW IS IT MADE* or Discovery Channel during the little free time that he has.

The rank structure of the non-officer cadre in the IAF progresses from Aircraftman with Technical Trade Classification II (AC II), Aircraftman with Technical Trade Classification I (AC I), Leading Aircraftman (LAC), Corporal (Cpl) and Sergeant (Sgt). Bhaurao cleared his AC II and AC I tests with 'Best in Trade' and 'Best Overall' distinction and was the only Aircraftman from his batch who passed out as AC I, while the others passed out as AC II. He had achieved a six-month head start over his batchmates. Six months later, he cleared his promotion examination to be promoted as LAC I.

Bhaurao got his first posting to BRMD, Kanpur in 1961. BRMD carried out repair and maintenance of all aircraft then in service with the IAF – Hunter, Mystere, Vampire, HF 24 Marut, Gnat, Ajeet, Canberra, B 24 J Liberator, Otter, Caribou, AN 12, IL 14, Vickers Viscount, Dakota and a host of other training and rotary wing aircraft. He was trained for repairs on Dakota, Vampire and Su 7 aircraft.

In 1962, Bhaurao was posted to AMD, Kanpur. AMD, precursor of HAL, was just beginning to manufacture Avro HS 748 transport aircraft under licence. Bhaurao has the distinction of being part of the flight testing team, from the electrical section, for the roll out of the maiden flight of the first three Avro manufactured at AMD. He recalls, "During the pre-flight checks of one of the Avro while checking the propeller actuator motor, one of the bolts broke while being tightened by me. The whole actuator motor had to be changed, and the maiden flight got delayed by three hours. I was supremely embarrassed."

The professional competence and communication skills of LAC Bhaurao Saraswat impressed his seniors, who recommended him for applying for Commission Officer training. It was 1963, and Bhaurao cleared his preliminary written test held at Kanpur. Thereafter, he was sent to Air Force SSB Center, Dehradun for PABT and Interview. The batch had 107 candidates, of which only two were serving personnel from IAF. Bhaurao was one of the seven candidates selected. Unfortunately, in the ensuing medical examination, he was declared unfit for pilot duty owing to leg length being half an inch less than the prescribed physical standards. He was, however, cleared for Navigator Branch. Here again he was heavily disappointed when there was no training course due for Navigators. By the time the course was announced he was overage for commission training.

Bhaurao was now detailed to attend one year Advanced Electrical training at No 4 Ground Training School at Bangalore. The course had an equivalence to a diploma. He once again got the distinction of being 'Best in Trade' and 'Best Overall.'

The innocuous sounding CPRS is a highly secretive special unit, which is directly attached to Operations Directorate at Air Headquarters Delhi, tasked with all important reprocessing of aerial photo reconnaissance data and aircraft gun camera photo record. In the mid-60s it was sub-divided into a Photo Reprocessing Section and a Modelling Section, headed by a Squadron Leader, comprised 50 plus personnel both from the IAF as well as civil specialists. Both the sections worked in water-tight compartments with duty-specific working hours. LAC Bhaurao Saraswat received his posting to CPRS in 1964. He was the sole tradesman for carrying out Electrical & Mechanical repairs and maintenance.

The photo reprocessing equipment held by CPRS was from Second World War vintage and had been left in a damaged state by the leaving Royal Air Force personnel and Indian origin servicemen who had opted for transfer to Pakistan during partition in 1947. It befell on Bhaurao to assist in first repairing and then ensuring serviceability of the vital equipment.

About the 1965 War with Pakistan, Bhaurao narrates with eagerness about one of their important achievements, "An aerial photo reconnaissance mission by Canberra aircraft over general area Chhamb revealed 40 to 50 numbers of thatched-hut structures in an open space. Subsequent confirmatory reconnaissance revealed changed GPRS locations of all the huts. It was highly unusual, and input was passed on to the Intelligence. One of their ground sources confirmed them to be Patton tanks. This resulted in the launch of air raids on the identified tank concentration."

By 1966, he got promoted to the rank of Corporal while still posted with CPRS. On completion of his tenure with CPRS in 1967, Bhaurao was selected along with four other specialists from different technical trades to undergo specialised training for repair and maintenance on the latest aircraft simulator for Su 7 fighter aircraft, in USSR. The second generation simulator was highly advanced for the times and could simulate 152 flight and armament parameters, except G-effects. After the initial fortnight of preliminaries in Moscow, the trainees spent the next seven months in the deep interiors of Kyrgyzstan, erstwhile USSR, learning about the equipment. A very strict security protocol veil shrouded the equipment, both in Russia as well as in India. Even the handwritten notes of the trainees had to be surrendered at the end of the working day, and on course completion were forwarded through diplomatic channels to the IAF representatives.

The Su 7 simulator, the most advanced in South East Asia in those days, was deployed at Adampur Airbase in Punjab by 1968. Bhaurao also received his posting to Adampur Airbase. He would spend the next five years training the fighter pilots on the aircraft simulator. Protracted exploitation of the simulator led to frequent malfunctioning, resulting in wrong inputs in ten percent of simulated landings. It was up to Bhaurao to identify the fault and modify the equipment. The modification met with the approval of the Russians and resulted in his receiving a commendation letter from his Commanding Officer.

The Indo-Pak War of 1971 led to exciting times at Adampur Air Base. The morale of the civil population was very high, and the IAF had the full support of the local populace as well as the civil administration. The arrest of two Pakistani spies along with their communication equipment was the talk of the surrounding areas and led to the forming of voluntary civil vigilance groups around the base. Squadrons of Hunter, Su 7 and MIG 21 were deployed on the base. The very first day of the war saw continuous air effort launched against Pakistan air and ground targets from 0600 hrs till beyond 1400 hrs. The skies around the base reverberated to the sounds of aircraft landing and taking off. The sounds of air raid warning sirens and tracers from the air defence guns lighting up the night skies became routine. Pakistan launched three to four airstrikes against Adampur Air Base during the entire war, but were unable to inflict any serious damage. In fact, it was the nearby village, Jandu Singha, which bore more of the brunt of PAF ire rather than the airbase.

In 1969, Bhaurao was promoted as Sgt with just 9 years of service against the average service of 12 years, the youngest in his batch to do so. In 1973, Bhaurao was detailed to attend six months technical training on SAM 2 long range missiles at Missile Training Institute, Baroda, in Gujarat. He was, thereafter, posted to 6 Wing Air Force at Barrackpore, as in-charge of Electrical repairs of the missiles.

Changing the Uniform

In July 1975, Bhaurao completed his stipulated service of 15 years with the IAF. He eagerly began looking forward to his second innings. As a graduate from Associate Member of Aeronautical Society of India (AMAeSI) completed in 1971, diploma in electrical engineering from Air Force and 15 years of distinguished work experience as electrical engineer with the IAF, he was ready to take the plunge in the rough and tumble of civil industry at the bright young age of 33 years. He had a whole life ahead of him.

During his two months leave pending retirement, Bhaurao applied for various jobs and appeared for several interviews. The job offers which he got in return were for guard duty, an affront to a technical man. Apparently, armed forces technical experience was not in great demand. After prolonged search for a technical opening, he was interviewed and selected by Walchandnagar Industry Ltd. (WIL), a heavy industry behemoth in defence, space, nuclear sector and engineering products manufacturing and with 2000-plus qualified engineers on its rolls. Here too he had a prolonged wait for the call letter. He had to face an interview with the General Manager, through intervention of a common acquaintance, before he got his appointment letter as a Junior Maintenance Engineer tasked with repairs and maintenance of lathes, furnaces and cranes. He joined WIL in the first week of August 1975 and was assigned challenging tasks from day one itself. Repair of a Coles crane, damaged in an accident 8 months ago, was the first work assignment for him. Says Bhaurao, "The crane required both electrical and mechanical repairs, but by evening I singlehandedly completed the repairs successfully, thanks to the expertise gained during my tenure with BRMD, Kanpur. This achievement brought me to the notice of the senior leadership of the company."

The first day success made Bhaurao the technical troubleshooter of his vertical and brought him his second assignment. He was now tasked to resolve the issue of frequent faults occurring in grinders on the floor shops and their consequent non-availability in adequate numbers. WIL used high-frequency and low-voltage grinders to avoid shock to users in the eventuality of leakage of electrical current from the equipment. These grinders were supplied by a USA-based company, were costly and not readily available. Informal surveys and discussions with site engineers by Bhaurao revealed an interesting root cause to the issue. Because the grinders were in short supply, the site engineers hoarded the good ones and used the unfit ones routinely. This led to an abnormally high down time of equipment and excessive requirement of spares and motor-winding materials. Based on his report, remedial actions were introduced and the problem was resolved for good.

As a troubleshooter, Bhaurao realised that it was advantageous to be forewarned of emerging technical crisis areas to enable effective and speedier response. In an organisation as large as WIL, reporting and decision making was a tedious process. At times, even small maintenance issues assumed crisis proportions necessitating urgent remedial actions. So he utilised his considerable communication skills to develop rapport with junior workers and shop in charges. This networking made him even more effective in dealing with critical technical repair and maintenance issues assigned to him for redress.

The biggest achievement of Bhaurao during his work with WIL was on a sensitive work assignment for KAPP. WIL was tasked to prepare a special seven metre-long shaft for KAPP. Raw material was imported from a foreign supplier, and machining was done in-house. Thereafter, it was required to be sent for heat treatment process, known as annealing, to HECL, Ranchi in Bihar. HECL was a government organisation with a weak work culture and had reported annual losses to the extent of rupees two hundred crores. A month went by without any progress in the annealing work at HECL campus. The project was being continuously monitored by PMO, and WIL was under tremendous pressure to accomplish the work on time. The management, already impressed with cross-domain functional skills of Bhaurao, dispatched him to beef up the WIL team at HECL. After studying the situation, he was able to identify the bottleneck as also key employees of HECL who could accomplish the task successfully. Thereafter he induced them, through payment for overtime work, to complete the work in the designated time frame.

WIL recognised the value of the professional expertise of Bhaurao by promoting him as Assistant Engineer and Senior Engineer in the second and fourth year of service, respectively. He was also privileged to consistently receive the highest bracket of annual increments.

In 1980, Bhaurao took a major decision of leaving WIL to join Kiran Spinning Mills at Thane and shifted to Mulund in central Bombay. Kiran Spinning Mills was a part of the Bharat Commerce and Industries Ltd. of Birla Group. The Mill had 3000 employees, 4 MW electric power consumption and diesel generators with electricity generation capacity of 3 MW.

Bhaurao had a hard time in getting adjusted to the unionised work environment of the textile manufacturing industry of Bombay. Then destiny intervened in the form of the Great Bombay Textile strike of 1982 in 65 textile mills by nearly 2,50,000 workers led by 'Doctorsahib' Datta Samant. The yearlong strike crippled most of the textile mills in Bombay. Kiran Spinning Mill had to be locked out, but Bhaurao along with key skeleton staff was retained till August 1984, when finally the mill was closed. He was left without a job. At this juncture, Mr Srikant Joshi, a very close friend of Bhaurao, advised him to become an entrepreneur.

Entrepreneur Projects and Consultancy

The process of manufacturing textile is spread over three stages. Spinning the fibres into yarns, weaving yarns to make fabric and fabric finishing. During the process of converting fibres into yarns, it is twisted to give it added strength. This twisting is to be set by a thermal process known as heat setting. The erstwhile large composite textile mills covered all the three stages. These mills disintegrated in the strike. To replace them, small textile units, specialising in one part of the manufacturing process, mushroomed all over Bombay.

Bhaurao surveyed the market and zeroed in on manufacturing heat setting chambers. The existing chambers were made of aluminium.

Bhaurao adopted an innovative approach by designing these chambers from stainless steel and also introduced automation in some of the processes, which was not there in the existing heat setting chambers. He sourced raw material from the open market and gave it to an external manufacturer along with specifications. The finished product, though costly, was sturdy and had the added advantage of automated process. The innovative design and high quality after sales service boosted the demand for the product designed by Bhaurao. The sale of the first prototype secured him 25 % returns on investment.

Buoyed by his initial success, Bhaurao set up Nisha Enterprise, named after his spouse. He used his savings to finance the business and quickly started manufacturing one heat setting chamber per month. By the end of the first year, Nisha Enterprise had generated an annual turnover of rupees five lakhs. A two-and-a-half time increase in annual income from his salary days.

Bhaurao assessed that the demand for his product would be short lived, so he started exploring avenues of entrepreneurship in the field of his core expertise, electrical engineering. Unfortunately, he suffered a slip disc in his vertebrae and was confined to bed for almost six months. The professional reputation of Bhaurao had come to the knowledge of Mr Arvind Biyani, proprietor of Damodar Synthetics Pvt. Ltd. at Tarapur, 120 km from Mulund in Mumbai. Mr Arvind Biyani hired Bhaurao as a consultant for his factory at Tarapur. In consideration of his medical condition, Bhaurao would be required to visit Tarapur only once a week for half a day.

After effecting full recovery from his slip disc condition, Bhaurao started undertaking electrical work contracts. By August 1984, he established Saraswat Engineering Services as a proprietary firm. His spouse, Nisha, assisted him with secretarial service and handling bank transactions.

Saraswat Engineering Services received its initial major breaks with Lavino Kapoor Ltd., Everest Kanto Cylinders Ltd., Orient Press Ltd., Samrudh Pharma Pvt. Ltd., reputed brands in Bombay. In the words of Bhaurao, "It was 1991 and Everest Kanto Cylinders Ltd. was in the process of revamping its existing capacity. The electrical project involved design, drawings, supply, installation, testing and commissioning of a transformer and 33 KV electrical sub-station, including cabling, panels and sub-panels. It was our first turnkey project and had overall value of rupees six crores. It has been our most satisfying project."

Within five years of its establishment, the firm achieved an annual turnover of a crore in rupees, and by 1997 it was three crores. It was also the year when his son Amit Saraswat joined the firm as a partner, and Saraswat Engineering Services was incorporated as a partnership firm. In a short time frame of ten years, Saraswat Engineering Services was able to establish business relationships with 50 to 60 firms.

Bhaurao recalls, "Our reputation and reliability bagged us a highly sensitive electro mechanical project with Bhabha Atomic Research Centre, in 2008-09, after signing a non-disclosure agreement. We executed the project over six to eight months. It gave me great pride to provide service to one of the premier institutions of our country."

It was closely followed by their first break in a foreign country when they were engaged by Bhageria Chemicals Ltd. as a consultant for supply, installation and commissioning of all electrical equipment work for Juhel Pharma project in Nigeria in 2009. "We hired manpower on a short-term contract and arranged all documentation, travel, on-site boarding and lodging for them. Being from the forces background, we went a step further to provide their families in India with organisational support. The last factor ensured undivided attention and dedication to work on hand by our contracted personnel," says Bhaurao.

The contract for the Arcelor Mittal coal mines and railway yard project in Liberia was awarded to Afcons Ltd., a Shapoorji Pallonji group company. A Canadian company was awarded consultancy for electrical work. Saraswat Engineering Services was engaged for supply of technical workforce and supervision of the electrical work on the site. The work had to be abruptly closed due to outbreak of Ebola epidemic in the region. Bhaurao then decided to concentrate on projects within India.

The electrical project for the Allahabad Airport was the one which tested to the hilt the innovative capabilities of Bhaurao and his team. The time frame for execution was very short; three spatially separated large structures needed to be electrically connected, the soil was prone to waterlogging, and it was monsoon time. External cabling and ducting work was difficult to execute. The project was very time sensitive, being linked to the Kumbha Mela and was being monitored by the PMO. In the words of Bhaurao, "Despite the monsoon-induced waterlogging, delay was simply not an option. The project had to be completed by December 2018. With literally hourly feedbacks to the PMO, the last few days felt like war room reporting. We had to put into use all our innovative skills to complete the project in time for the Kumbha Mela of 2019, which was witness to the largest human gathering on earth."

Sgt Bhaurao Saraswat is now nearing 80 years of age but is still sprightly and energetic. He has good reason to be satisfied with his entrepreneur journey as he prepares to hand over the baton of his premium business venture to the next generation, his son Amit Saraswat. Bhaurao, nevertheless, plans to remain active in business advisory role.

BHAURAO SPEAKS

Learnings from the IAF

Recently, while reminiscing about my life and career on my 50th wedding

anniversary, I recalled that the best phase of my life were the 15 years with the IAF. I hold them to be my most precious and prized years with the fondest memories.

But for my service with the IAF, I could not have undertaken this marathon journey as an entrepreneur. My communication skills, courage of conviction, self-discipline and integrity are a result of my service with the IAF.

Even my technical expertise is much more than I could have achieved working in the civil industry. I had access to high technology equipment, a well-stocked technical library and comprehensive manuals.

Minimising downtime of precious equipment is fundamental to Air Force repair and maintenance process. Speed and dexterity in repairs and maintenance becomes second nature of the Air Force technicians. The chart system based Quality Assurance Plan of the Air Force is the bible in Saraswat Engineering Services.

Major Achievements

Undertaking project work for BARC is undeniably our greatest achievement. Being a highly committed organisation, only the best is acceptable to them. Getting repeat projects from them enhanced our self-esteem and brand image.

Technically speaking, our most satisfying project was the turnkey project for Everest Kanto Cylinders. Their engineers wanted a 150-metre-long buss duct which, as per the manufacturers of buss duct equipment, had not been tried out in India due to issues of vibrations, expansion and distortion. We took up the challenge and also offered two years guarantee. The complex looking issue had a very simple solution, incorporating expansion joints every 30 metres. Quarter of a century later, the buss duct is still functional.

Electrical project of Allahabad Airport is also one of our biggest achievements because of the volume, technical complexity and time available to complete the project.

Future Vision

We plan to expand the scope of our rated project undertaking capability from 5 crores for government projects and 15 crores for corporate sector projects. We are looking at options of acquisition or merger to achieve our aim. Already we have acquired stake holding in Prashant Electricals Ltd. to expand the scope and volume of our business.

Advice for the Mad Vets

The ideal age for starting an entrepreneur venture is 35 to 40 years to maximise possibility of success.

The veterans should maintain mental robustness in the highly competitive business world. Maintaining a conducive work floor environment, ensuring strong financial position, recovery of dues and regulatory compliances require great attention to detail.

Personnel with defence background, relatively, have greater chances of success in entrepreneurship because of their dedication and sincerity of approach.

Maintain your business documents well, and don't shy away from your tax payments. When you are looking for bank loans, your balance sheet and tax payments are crucial documents.

Options for the Mad Vets to Undertake New Ventures

Services sector is ideally suited to the temperament of veterans. But please stick to the line you know best and is closest to your interest.

Philosophy Towards Life

Man is born to work, work and work.

Nothing has been more inspiring than the Sanskrit shloka:

> "Karagre vaste Lakshmi, Karmadhye Saraswati;
> Karmule tu Govind, Prabhate kardarshanam."

It means that Lakshmi rests at the tip of hand, Saraswati at the base of hand and Govind in the centre of hand. Lakshmi being on tip of the hands may slip out of hand, but Saraswati is at the base of the hand and would remain with you lifelong. Govind rests at the middle of the palm to signify that He keeps equal distance from wealth and knowledge.

I look forward to leaving this world while still at work, on my own two feet.

Personal Qualities that Have Helped

I have always been interested in reading the literary works of Swami Vivekanand, and my friends too have similar interests.

Personal integrity and loyalty to my country are the two pillars of faith for me.

The Future of India

There is greater social awareness and increased per capita earnings. Coupled with 'Make in India,' we have a very bright future. India would be a driving force for services sector and most importantly the "Spiritual Capital" of the world.

One Mantra for the Mad Vets

Take up your entrepreneurship with whole heart. There is no end to 'ifs and buts.'

Willingness to Mentor Mad Vets

Always ready.

I have promoted a few already, and they are doing exceedingly well.

On Role of Spouse

Nisha is my backbone. Though she is a matriculate by education, her keen sense of support and understanding the emotional side of my venture far superseded her qualifications. She was active in the social circles and family welfare events of the Air Force community. I would be nothing today had it not been for her support in all times, even and odd. She was highly supportive of my decision to become an entrepreneur. She was and still is the mirror of my decisions. In fact, she went a step further and provided secretarial services during the startup stage of my venture and subsequently supervised my office staff. She keeps a diligent watch over company finances and payments.

She is also an active member of the local Lion's Club.

* * *

An all-encompassing essay, with a poetic licence, on the simplicity of theory and the difficulty of practice of leadership.

LEADERSHIP

Leadership is the art of influencing people
To voluntarily accept you as the group leader.
They follow the treads you have made
Or move fearlessly on the path indicated by you.
Accepting your destination as their goal,
Making the impossible possible on your say so.

To be a leader is not so simple;
You sweat and toil along with the led.
You feel the group and have a feel for the group,
Their sweat your care, their blood your loss.
You know their pulse, you voice their thoughts,
Their fear you sense, you predict their gait.

Their sorrow is yours, your joy they share,
The store of energy comes from you.
In adversity you must stand tall,
Head held high, shoulders square, the voice all firm.
Your entering the arena must make the difference,
It is the belief in you that holds the group.

The decision is yours, the action theirs,
All gains are theirs, you own up to the loss.
The reins that you handle guide the group,
The whip that you wield firms the group.
Leadership is gentleness with a ruthless streak,
For the cause of the group culling you do.

Leadership is an iron fist in velvet gloves,
It's not for the squeamish that's for sure.
Vindictiveness, cruelty, selfishness and frailty
Will definitely ensure the leader's fall.
Decisiveness, firmness, character, generosity,
Humility, wit and wisdom are the leader's demand.

And how do you know that the leader has arrived?
You must read the signs to know of that.
The group voluntarily forms where the leader stands,
And it's the look in their eyes that says it all.
The mind is one and so are the thoughts,
Because the leader and the led have merged into one.

- Col RS Sidhu

* * *

A Unique Army Navy Veterans Jointmanship Venture: Niche Risk Consultancy Service

We are used to listening very hierarchically. In today's VUCA world we need to listen 360 degrees; you never know—the game-changing suggestion might come from most unexpected quarters.

- Lt Cdr Pawan Desai

MitKat Advisory Services Pvt. Ltd. (MitKat) is a unique venture in many ways. On the face of it, the name, *per se*, appears to be a little frivolous for a corporate venture occupying a niche section in the new age information and consulting sector. On closer scrutiny, it emerges that the name 'MitKat' – an acronym for 'Mitigating Knowledge Age Threats' – expresses the full spectrum of their operational domain. It's their USP.

Set up by two of the most highly qualified professionals from IA and IN, with extensive corporate experience, it synergises the widest spectrum of maritime and land space skills, knowledge and experience in their chosen field of commercial operations. An unheard of jointmanship in the Indian corporate sector.

It is also unique that the co-founders ceded leadership space in their corporate governance structure by inviting a leading domain expert as Chairman on their Board of Governors.

Incorporated in 2010 at Mumbai, now a decade later, MitKat is Asia's leading risk consultancy, has its own AI-enabled Intelligence Platform, advising more than 50 of the world's top 100 global corporations and has executed projects in more than 25 countries across 5 continents. With offices pan India and in Singapore, annual revenue of couple of million US Dollars, it is profitable and debt-free. And even the global Covid-19 pandemic has not been able to dent their spirits. Their growth and progress continues unabated.

MitKat has the singular distinction of conducting enterprise-wide security audits, covering hundreds of locations. It envisions, designs and operates National/Regional/Global Command and Control Centres for leading global banks, IT and infrastructure companies and conglomerates. It also provides implementation and oversight support on complex security projects in challenging environments in Africa, West Asia, South & South East Asia, China, Japan and Australia, while its embedded security leaders support some of the world's most famous organisations in Technology, Finance, Consulting & Manufacturing domains.

MitKat has also been knowledge partner to nearly 100 security events and its leaders have been invited to speak across 20 countries including key economic centres such as New York, San Francisco, London, Brussels, Dubai, Bangkok, Beijing, Jakarta, Singapore and most of South Asia.

To understand the synergy brought into their joint venture by Col S M Kumar, aka Sam, and Lt Cdr Pawan Desai, CISA (Certified Information Security Auditor), CISSP (Certified Information Systems Security Professional), CBCP (Certified Business Continuity Planner), the co-founders of MitKat Advisory, it would be worthwhile to first have an understanding of the learnings they realised in their respective pre-entrepreneurial lives.

COL S M KUMAR (Sam)

It was the 4th of July 1986 that 2/Lt Samrendra – translates as 'King of Battle' in Hindi – Mohan Kumar, very proud of his name, a new star on his shoulder and countless stars in his eyes was reporting for duty as a newly commissioned officer to his assigned unit 9th Battalion, the Mechanised Infantry Regiment. During the first interaction over lunch with his senior subaltern Capt Varinder Singh, 2/Lt Samrendra Mohan Kumar proudly gave out his full rank and name. The wise

and discerning Capt Varinder Singh immediately declared that the name was too long and said that Sammy would be the name he would answer to hereafter. A stunned Samrendra protested. But Virender sternly gave out his very simple logic, that pronouncing his long sounding name prior to passing orders on radio would mean losing valuable time in battle and that was going to be unacceptable in a Paltan with many Battle Honours, Gallantry Awards and Commendations! The subdued subaltern then humbly requested any name other than Sammy. Veeroo, with a glint in his eye said, "OK you are Sam," a name that stuck with him for life. The last nail to this narrative was hammered when after marriage even his spouse joined in calling him Sam. "Rank continued to increase, but Sam remained just Sam" is how he ruefully expresses his evident disappointment even to this day.

Sam was the youngest of three sons in a family that hails from Kumar Bajitpur village in the historic district of Vaishali in Bihar, known to be home to the first democracy in the world around 6th century BC. His father was a professor and mother a homemaker.

Military Training

Sainik School Tilaiya was deemed to be one of the best schools in Bihar. A bright student, Sam appeared for the entrance examination, cleared it and joined the school in 1976. During the penultimate year at the school, Sam appeared and qualified for the NDA, Khadakvasla entrance examination and joined the academy in the year 1982.

Sam was a bundle of nerves as he entered the hallowed portals of NDA. Coming from a rural background and exposed to English only from sixth standard onwards, he felt overawed by the polished mannerisms, self-confidence and English conversational skills of his fellow new cadets, coming from some of the most renowned schools of India, children with privileged upbringings and sons of very senior officers from the three services. Dressed in their jeans and Polo Ts, most seemed more polished and accomplished.

But it all changed dramatically. The mandatory visit to the barber shop and the issue of Khaki and Olive Greens clothing was all it took to demolish all outwardly differences.

In a sense, the playing field had been levelled in the first 24 hours.

NDA is where the cadets from all the three services – Army, Air Force and Navy – receive joint training for three years before graduating on to pre-commission training institutes of their respective Services. Friendships made here last a lifetime and form the bedrock of inter-service cooperation in later years.

Sam's humble background, which seemingly appeared to be a drawback, now gave him an edge over the other cadets. The inherent toughness, a gift from his formative years, stood Sam in good stead, enabling him to take to the rigours of military training like fish to water. In June 1985, his final year in NDA, Sam was privileged to receive the Chiefs of Staff Championship Banner on behalf of Echo Squadron, the Champion Squadron, from Shri Rajiv Gandhi, the then Prime Minister.

Three years of rigorous training at NDA and another year of tough army training at IMA, Dehradun, and Sam was ready to be commissioned into the IA. The grit, determination and sheer competence, coupled with excellent academic performance in topping academics and service subjects, outstanding performance in sports by being the champion boxer in his weight category and an exceptional cross-country runner enabled Sam to not only overcome his background handicap but also outperform his batchmates to be awarded with the 'Sword of Honour' for being the best all-round Gentleman Cadet, as well as the 'President's Gold Medal' for standing first in the order of merit.

Sam recalls, "On 14 June, 1986, when my batch 78 Regular and 61 Technical passed out from IMA, I can still vividly remember the day as if it was yesterday. As I commanded the passing out parade, my parents, including my mother, all of 8th class pass, but a woman with immense wisdom, sat in the first row on the first two seats; there was a great sense of accomplishment – 'Where you started from did not matter; what you accomplished and achieved, did.'"

Life in the Army

Life with the battalion was exciting. Knowing of his boxing credentials, he was made in charge of the unit boxing team. While involved in light sparring during training of boxers, one of the boxers suddenly became aggressive in his blows. Sam realised there was something amiss. Without second thoughts, Sam dug into his skills and nearly knocked down the reputed boxer. And then everything came back to normal. Sam had passed his first test in the eyes of the troops he was to command. That day he learnt that you have to be better than the troops in all spheres of professional competence to earn their respect. It was this drive to excel that made him achieve career highs by topping various professional courses he attended. Sam also achieved the distinction of being graded the best student in Driving & Maintenance Instructor Course, Best in Special Mission during Commando Course and achieved a Distinguished Grade (D) on Tank Technology Course.

The only army officer from his batch, Sam was selected to attend the prestigious Advanced Command and Staff Course at Joint Services Command & Staff College, Bracknell, with residence at Camberley,

United Kingdom. This was not only a professional high, but a turning point in his life. On landing at Heathrow Airport on his way to attend the staff course, Sam was struck by the 'dignity of labour' and the fact of 'no work being too small.' Multi-racial and multicultural interactions with over 300 students from more than ninety countries was an experience of a lifetime. Battlefield tours to USA and Normandy, France and another visit to the US, including stay and training at Infantry School at Fort Benning, which had a 1600 m running track and an international airport within the campus, Air Strike Command, Langley, the largest Naval Base in the world at Norfolk, Virginia and briefings by top officials in Washington DC, served to broaden the mental horizon and realise the enormous scale of operations of the armed forces of USA, the then undisputed Global Leader and Superpower. Learnings derived during this course equipped Sam with skill sets and knowledge which he would use successfully during his entrepreneurship venture.

In a mobile battle, it is inherent for the Mechanised Forces to invariably gravitate to the point of decision. A Combat Group of Mechanised Forces, comprising fifty to hundred armoured fighting vehicles with dedicated aviation, artillery, engineering, communication and logistic support – is one of the most lethal and potent forces on the battlefield designed to inspire 'shock and awe' in the minds of the enemy. A Combat Group, by design, is agile and flexible, with frequent groupings and regroupings being the norm, enabling it to accomplish the assigned operational mission in a fast and fluid battlefield – a virtue much required for success in a VUCA business world of today. The speed of movement coupled with the destructive firepower at the disposal of a Combat Group bludgeons the enemy into submission either through shock and awe or physical destruction. History is replete with examples where Mechanised Forces are known to have paralysed the minds of the enemy commander, forcing the enemy to surrender without a fight. Sam had risen in rank to beget the coveted command of such an outfit. The flamboyance and mental mobility developed during this command has stood Sam in good stead, as also firmed his belief that in an era of increasing risks "agile eco-systems are the way of the future."

It is the dream of every fighting arm officer to command the unit he is commissioned into. It was true for Sam as well. After successfully completing the command of his battalion, Sam decided to hang his uniform graciously, while he was at the peak of his career. In Sam's words, "My cherished dream was accomplished. My days of direct command were over. I wanted to leave on a high. Having commanded the Passing Out Parade on the first day of my service, having had an opportunity to represent my country overseas at the Command and Staff Course, having done all the ticks thus far, a grand farewell by most of the 800 men, with whom I had spent two decades of my life, seemed to be the logical way and the apt moment to bid farewell to arms. My Army Unit had indeed been my home for 21 years, and the bonds still remain strong. Even if I forget my birthday or wedding anniversary, my Unit does not, even when deployed in extreme high altitude or UN Mission overseas." Sam's Army Discharge Book reads his permanent address as: Col S M Kumar, 9 MECH INF (7 GRENADIERS), c/o 56 APO. I asked Sam why. He said while leaving his unit for good after hanging his uniform, he did not realise he ever had another home or permanent address.

In 2007, after 21 years of meritorious service and a dream career, Sam bade farewell to the army – a decision which surprised his friends in the army and even his wife and close family. He was ready for the second innings, though not yet sure of the option he would exercise.

Managing the Transition

Sam received referral-based invitations from a leading conglomerate foraying into Organised Retail, which appeared to be a sunshine industry then, and from Mahindra SSG to appear for interview. While he liked the kind of work which Mahindra SSG offered, to raise a business unit around Security and Governance Consulting, and the CEO was insistent that he take up the offer and join immediately after leaving, Sam did not feel adequately prepared. So he undertook a six-month management course at Indian Institute of Management, Calcutta, one of the top B-Schools and joined Mahindra SSG after completing the program in October 2007.

Raising a business sub-unit was a rich entrepreneurial experience for Sam. There was a bit of initial struggle for him, as he thought that everything from market conditions, to bad customers and not so good HR, Marketing & Sales support were responsible for his poor performance. It took a few months into the job for Sam to accept that the problem was within him. He then got down to listening to customers, understanding, appreciating and analysing business and market dynamics better, before coming up with some innovative products and offerings with useful guidance from his CEO, also a distinguished veteran.

Around this point of time, Sam began carpooling with a former Naval Officer Pawan Desai, a submariner and an engineer who specialised in information security and resiliency and led that vertical. Though having different skill sets, they shared very similar values, including empathy, love and respect for their teams, innovative approach and some risk-taking ability. They hit it off well, courtesy time-consuming commutes associated with Mumbai, an island mega-city of over 20 million people with limited road space and long working hours associated with the consulting profession. They were destined to go a long way together in their later life.

2008 happened to be the year of one of the worst global recessions as also a life-changing event – 26/11 terror attacks, where Sam and Pawan, with some of their team members spent most of their time in and around Taj and Oberoi Hotels. Mahindra SSG, the first serious home-grown risk consultancy, saw great demand for risk assessments and strengthening corporate security. Post 26/11 terror attacks, Sam's business unit witnessed phenomenal growth despite the ongoing global recession and hired some very bright and talented ex-armed forces young officers. His team also gave a good account of themselves in some very challenging assignments, which involved the aftermath of a rocket attack on a corporate in NE India and an industrial accident in Chhattisgarh, receiving solid appreciation from very tall industry leaders.

Phase I of the transition was complete. But while Sam's business unit was flourishing, it was profitable and debt-free; global recession was throwing a pall of general gloom on the market. It was time to move on.

LT CDR PAWAN DESAI

In the peak of summer of June 1997, at SSB, Bhopal, thirty-six young aspirants, vying for the Short Service Commission into the Technical Graduate Entry Scheme of the Indian Navy, were waiting with bated breath for the declaration of the results. They had undergone one of the most exhaustive selection processes to gauge their power of expression, effective intelligence and reasoning, organising and influencing ability, social adaptability and cooperation, sense of responsibility and initiative, determination and stamina, courage and self-confidence, speed of decision and dynamism, through nearly three dozen written and practical tests, by a team of domain experts, to analyse their suitability to be a Gentleman and an Officer of the IN. The widely used corporate terminology of 360-degree review pales into insignificance in comparison to the scrutiny these candidates had undergone. Their intelligence, emotional and social quotients, thought processes, response to stimulus, their very life had been studied threadbare, over these past five days.

The result was declared, and only one candidate had successfully negotiated the labyrinthine selection process. He was Pawan Desai, and, overnight he became a celebrity in the eyes of the other aspirants. By a quirk of circumstance, owing to the absence on duty of a medical specialist, he perforce had to stay another two weeks at the SSB location to undergo the mandatory Board for Medical Examination. All new incoming candidates, and there were aplenty, approached him for consultation on the *mantras* for success in the SSB. Pawan happily obliged; he had discovered his true calling. The future Risk Mitigation Consultant had been born.

Pawan, the elder of two brothers, was born in 1974, into a family that hailed from Rajpipla in District Bharuch of Gujarat. Right from his early childhood, he felt an attraction for ships, to the extent of purchasing ships as toys. As his father was employed with a medical company, Pawan was brought up in Ahmedabad, New Delhi and Vadodara. After a few years, his father started a surgical equipment manufacturing unit that specialised in neurosurgery equipment. Pawan completed his schooling from New Delhi and Vadodara and Bachelors in Metallurgy Engineering from Maharaja Siyaji Rao University in 1995.

A sports enthusiast, Pawan was enamoured with playing cricket, a game in which he specialised as a spin bowler and batsman. With support from his parents, Pawan spent more time on sports fields than behind a study desk. So it was no surprise when he qualified in open selections to join the Indian Oil Corporation Under-15 Cricket Team. Subsequently, he was also a member of the Cricket Team of Faculty of Technology, Maharaja Siyaji Rao University. Life to him was all about playing.

Pawan enjoyed a laidback lifestyle; in fact, he was a procrastinator. But his demeanour changed completely on the sports field, where he was highly combative. This twin-faceted personality would often be pointed out by his family and friends. But he revelled in on-field competitive behaviour. This behavioural pattern soon developed into a rebellious streak against authority in sports. As a result, he would often walk away from established cricket teams and create new ones.

On completion of his graduation in Engineering, Pawan worked in Quality Control in two different firms in Ankleshwar and Ahmedabad, before realising that he was not enthused with Engineering. So when his mother showed him an advertisement for joining the Navy, he instantly jumped at the opportunity. In the interim, while waiting for the announcement of the merit list for entry into the Navy, he also secured admission in an MBA (Master's in Business Administration) course in

GH Patel Institute of Management, Vidyanagar near Anand in Gujarat. It was here that he developed mutual attraction for one of his batchmates, Noopur, whom he would marry two years later.

After a month's stint with MBA, Pawan received the call letter for joining the IN. Without any second thoughts, he quit the MBA course and joined training for IN. Like on the sports fields, he did not believe in going the conventional way. Since almost everyone in Gujarat would have chosen MBA, he charted a different course.

Military Training

Goa was at its hot and humid best in August of 1997 when Pawan with his regulation size black box reached the Main Gate of INS Mondovi where he was to undergo basic military training for the next six months. Dropped at the gate, he was uncertain how to arrange help in carrying the black box. Unfamiliar with military practices, he committed his first of a series of *faux pas*. He asked a senior-term cadet, loitering nearby, to help in carrying the box. After a curious stare, the cadet obliged. Pawan spent the next few days paying for this obligation through profuse sweat and tears. The decision was his, so Pawan had no choice but to bear it through.

On completion of basic training, Pawan moved on to INS Shivaji, Lonavla for his marine engineering curriculum, for the next four months. Being a good sportsman, Pawan easily cleared his swimming test the first time. Only three other batchmates managed to do the same. It appeared that all Navy personnel being good at swimming was a myth. He was promptly assigned the additional responsibility to ensure all failing cadets pass their swimming test. So, in the chilly winters of Lonavla, he would be spending his mornings and off time in the cold waters of the outdoor swimming pool while his batchmates relaxed. It was some time before he realised the senior trainees' acronym for the Navy – "Never Again Volunteer Yourself."

Training at INS Shivaji was followed by short training capsules at INS Hamla at Mumbai and INS Venduruthi. Sub Lt Pawan Desai was now ready to receive his first posting.

Life in the Navy

Outside the human race, a wolf pack is the most ruthless and efficient fighting body. It is extremely difficult for a prey to survive pursuit by a pack of wolves in the wild. No wonder, a group of hunter killer submarines, one of the most efficient and deadliest marine platforms, is loosely referred to as a 'Wolf Pack.' During the Second World War, they were credited with sinking the maximum number of marine vehicles. Unseen, unheard, cut off from the known world, not knowing day or night, they prowl the depths of marine waters, for days, weeks and months, ever scanning their surroundings, without letting their guard down – even for an instant. Once deployed on battle station, the submarine has to be completely self-reliant on onboard resources for its very survival.

The living and work stations for the crew are highly cramped and claustrophobic, requiring the highest levels of mental robustness and supreme physical fitness. It requires men with nerves of steel and faith in their own professional competency, a special breed of men, to be able to withstand the mental and physical rigours of a prolonged tour of operational submarine duty. Only volunteers can join the submarine service. Every volunteer has to successfully undergo a two-tier test. First is the physical ability to withstand barometric overpressure, which has a failure rate of 30% to 40%. The second is mental robustness to withstand the claustrophobic environment by crawling through a cramped horizontal tunnel, opening an escape valve, easing the body into a narrow 30 metre-high water channel and floating up to the surface, in pitch-dark conditions and in full hydro gear. The dropout rate is approximately 20%.

This is the reason why 'Dolphin badge of the Submariners' is the most coveted insignia of the Indian Navy. The inherent urge to be with the best made Sub Lt Pawan Desai to volunteer for Submarine service, clear the qualifying tests and be posted as Assistant Engineer Officer on board INS Sindhukriti, a Kilo Class Submarine with home port at Mumbai.

His onboard training on INS Sindhukriti would prove to be invaluable in later life as an entrepreneur. As a Submariner you have to not only master your domain but also have functional knowledge of all other spheres, as your own and your submarine mates' life could depend on cross-domain functioning during crisis. This was a lesson which he would carry through to his second career successfully.

At the close of his seven-year short service contract, Pawan opted for release from naval service. Life beyond onboard submarines held no challenges for him and appeared monotonous. He was willing to explore new challenges outside the Navy.

Managing Change of Uniform

While still in service, Pawan utilised his spare time to successfully earn his Masters in Management from Jamna Lal Bajaj Institute of Management Studies, Mumbai, one of the top B-Schools in India. While looking around for a suitable offer, he received a call from Mahindra Special Services Group (Mahindra SSG), for working in the Information Security Consulting domain. The interview lasted for an hour on a Saturday in July of 2004, and by the time he reached home in Colaba, Pawan already had the offer letter in hand. He joined it as a consultant in 2004, thus commencing his corporate journey of learning, unlearning and re-learning.

Says Pawan, "The biggest adjustment I had to make was hearing 'NO' from subordinates. In their eyes, I was raw and did not know the nuances of my role. The first six months were difficult. But I soon realised that I had four major advantages working for me. First, information security is inbuilt in the armed forces, so it was not a new subject for me. Second, being an Engineer I was comfortable with Technology. Third, having done my MBA in Information Technology, management was not an issue. Finally, my armed forces experience had imparted adequate leadership skills to leverage my environment."

Pawan quickly settled into his new environment, learnt the intricacies of the profession and cleared three major global certifications, CISA, CIISP, and CBCP.

Through hands-on experience, he learnt nearly everything that was to be learnt from the lowest level upwards. Slowly and steadily, Pawan created leadership space for himself within the organisation.

"Attrition in my organisation worked in my favour," says Pawan. "I volunteered for responsibilities held by those leaving leadership roles, while others were not willing to look at lateral growth in newer disciplines. So in four years, I was handling operations nearly accounting for 80% of the organisation's revenues. The company senior leadership was visionary and forward looking and continuously pushed boundaries for new ideas and innovations. The thrill of creativity fuelled my growth and allowed me to remain loyal to the organisation for seven years."

Pawan Meets Sam

It took some coaxing for Pawan to open about his first meeting with Sam. "It was late 2007 and I was away on a project. When I returned after a week, to my surprise, the organisation was abuzz with talk about a Sam. In the space of a week, Sam had been able to occupy the leadership space which I felt was mine. So I thought, *Who the hell is he?* But once we started interacting, trust developed instantaneously and we became the best of friends. I helped his transitioning in finance and project management and visualisation domains. He took me through the paces of looking at the larger picture, conflict management and strategic understanding. I had grown bottom up, and he learnt to descend, unlearn and relearn. Then we grew up together."

Late 2009/early 2010 was to be a time of cataclysmic changes in the life of Pawan and Sam. There was a change in senior leadership in Mahindra SSG, and their idea of success changed. Pawan had peaked in the organisation, and the restless energy of Sam, whose business was growing rapidly while the rest of world was still reeling from the shock of economic recession, was looking at a horizon beyond Mahindra SSG. The two would often discuss the affront of foreign organisations occupying business risk consultancy space in India. It almost became an ego issue, which over a period of time got converted into a joint dream of creating a world-class Indian risk advisory firm.

Sam was the first to fire the salvo, still not sure what to do. He also appeared for couple of interviews but heard nothing from the prospective employers. Then one fine day, Sam decided to be an entrepreneur.

Sam had come to rely on the business instincts of Pawan and wanted him on board for the planned startup. Sam also had confidence in the astute business sense of Noopur and went about convincing her of the possibilities of success in their own risk management venture. Once she was on board, Pawan, himself looking at newer pastures as was his wont, readily accepted to join.

In the words of Pawan, "Ironically, immediately after he had decided to go on his own and invited me in, Sam got a couple of too-good-to-be-true job offers; even during those recessionary times we were in demand. But, Sam being Sam, once he had made up his mind and invited me in, there was no looking back. I was surprised at the ease with which he said no to those offers and stayed on course over the next decade. Selection and Maintenance of Aim, Sam often reminds me, is the first and most important Principle of War. Thereafter, we have remained committed to our vision of creating a truly world-class Risk Consultancy."

Mitkat Advisory Services Pvt. Ltd.

Sam and Pawan are opposites and yet complementary in their personality, skills and domain expertise. Pawan's strength lies in financial and project management. Sam's forte is in Strategic Understanding and Marketing. Sam is skilled in exuding flamboyancy of the Mechanised Forces and promising the moon to open doors, while Pawan employs the aura of quiet competency of a Submariner to keep the door open by delivering the moon. The former personifies cockiness through competence, while the latter projects confidence through competency. It is this synergy of opposites which sets them apart from the crowd and makes them a name to reckon with.

Sam and Pawan were not knowledgeable about the intricacies involved in establishing a company, so they bought a 35 % partnership in a non-operative company Mitkat Ventures. Once they were confident enough, they decided to set up their own enterprise.

MitKat Advisory Services was incorporated as Private Limited Company with the Registrar of Companies on 31 August 2010 with Corporate Office at Mumbai, as a premium Risk Consultancy, for mitigating operational risks in Cyber, Geopolitical, Socio-Economic, Technology, Infrastructure, Regulatory, Environmental, Safety and Security domains. Col S M Kumar, ex-Indian Army and Lt Cdr Pawan Desai, CISA, CISSP, CBCP, BCCP, ex-Indian Navy were the co-founders. They also had a third co-founder from a Big 4 Consulting firm whose worldview, as they discovered, was slightly different from theirs. Eventually, they bought out his stakes completely after a year.

Pawan recalls, "We used to be really hungry for success. One of our first assignments materialised from a telephonic call from a financial institute in Gurgaon to carry out a Technical Surveillance Counter Measure of their Boardroom in Gurgaon. Expression of interest was required to be given by 1700 hrs the same day. Sam, based in Mumbai, learning of it around 1100 hrs from a former colleague and friends, flew down from Mumbai to Delhi, asked a friend to chauffer him and was on the company premises 15 minutes prior to the confirmation deadline. The Director of the company was really impressed and awarded the assignment to us. Sam then got down to organising the manpower and technical equipment for the task at hand through the night and commenced delivery the next morning."

The company started with advisory services in domains as diverse as HR, Risk and Technology. However, within six months, Pawan and Sam learnt the importance of focus and excellence in whatever they did. To this day, FOCUS or as Lt Gen Sudhir Sharma, Chairman of MitKat Advisory puts it, "Do less to do more" remains one of the MitKat's core mantras.

MitKat expanded its national and regional footprints by opening offices in Gurgaon, part of Delhi National Capital Region, in 2011 and

Bangalore in 2013. The company extended its geographical presence internationally in 2012, by establishing an office in Singapore.

2012 was a decisive year for the nascent organisation in many ways. Pawan and Sam parted ways with their third Partner. Lt Gen Sudhir Sharma PVSM, AVSM, YSM, VSM joined the Board of Directors as Chairman, and a very bright and experienced entrepreneur Parag Agarwal joined the company as a Director. Cmde (Dr) Prem Chand, a distinguished Naval veteran, alumnus of Indian Institute of Technology Madras, Indian School of Business, PhD in Cyber Security from Birla Institute of Technology & Science Pilani, and a former Chief Information Officer of Tech Mahindra, also joined the company as Executive Vice Chairman a year later. As the world rebounded from the Lehman Crisis, the top lines and bottom lines also grew, and as MitKat grew in reputation, top-of-the-line talent from the best colleges became easy to find.

Soon after Lt Gen Sudhir Sharma, a visionary with deep networking skills and rich global exposure, joined Board of Directors of MitKat as the Chairman, he coined the slogan, "Do less to do more," based on the army war fighting principles of "concentration of force and economy of effort," whereby combat force is concentrated on a focal point thus synergising kinetic energy in developing momentum to overcome enemy resistance in a faster time frame and by employing minimum resources. In corporate parlance, identify and focus on core skills, enabling development of greater expertise leading to enhanced quality of operational delivery, thereby capturing a wider spectrum of targeted market. It minimises operational expenditure and generates greater revenue, thus maximising return on investment. In accordance with this thought process, the company realigned its operations to focus on Intelligence, Physical Security & Safety, Cyber Security, Resilience and Crisis Management, the complete spectrum of security and risk advisory services.

Lt Gen Sudhir Sharma, as a Brigadier, was posted as Military Advisor at India's High Commission in London when he first came across Sam who had come to United Kingdom to attend the yearlong prestigious Advanced Command and Staff Course at Joint Services Command &

Staff College, Bracknell, with residence at Camberley, United Kingdom. Lt Gen Sharma, himself an alumnus of Staff College Camberley, supported and mentored Sam during this period. The two developed a mutual respect and regard for each other during this period.

On being asked what made a senior General agree to join a then unproven organisation, his response was "In India, Risk Mitigation was a wholly untested idea at that point of time. Sam and Pawan had shown great courage of conviction in coming out of their comfort zone and undertaking huge economic risk by starting MitKat in an unproven market segment. When Sam requested me to join MitKat, I had several lucrative post-retirement offers from the Government and Corporate world. But his passion, integrity, single-minded focus on quality and, above, all business ethics inspired me to join him at MitKat. Of course, mutual rapport, the challenge and love for entrepreneurship, too, played a key role in my decision." About his idea of measuring the success of MitKat, he says, "We have the highest ethical standards in the market, and I have substantive experience to say so with full confidence. We occupy a niche segment in our domain due to our focus on quality and desire to be best in class. MitKat has imbibed the best of the underlying ethos of the armed forces and strongly believes in the pursuit of excellence. It therefore is no surprise that our customer satisfaction indices are very high, and the same reflects in our balance sheet with more than 90% repeat business."

Parag Agarwal too contributed immensely with his great business sense and huge entrepreneurial experience. He is now more involved with a social enterprise JanaJal, which is probably the first Indian social venture to receive foreign direct investment.

What strikes me about MitKat is its organisational culture, great energy and its ability to stay ahead of the curve. When Covid-19 struck, MitKat decided that its employees would work from home nearly two weeks before it became commonplace. MitKat's young Intel analysts, also popularly called as "Corona Warriors," rose up to the challenge of keeping the clients and the community updated. As a goodwill measure,

MitKat offered weeks of complimentary advisory services to many organisations. When India was locked down for a few weeks, MitKat seamlessly switched to online working and training.

Today the company, with over hundred employees on its rolls and its own AI assisted portal, is a leader in Asia in Corporate Intelligence and Travel Risk Management Services. It also provides corporate intelligence alerts and advisories to leading global companies. MitKat has a best-in-class team of Intel and research analysts with education and degrees from the world's best universities. Apart from a very capable and experienced management team, it has a top-class team of consultants from diverse backgrounds specialising in Security Consulting & Design, Cyber Security, Technology and Fraud Risk Management. MitKat attracts and retains best-in-class talent and is an equal opportunities employer with the women outnumbering men in two business units, something unprecedented in the security domain.

Over the years, MitKat has attracted some other very capable veterans to join the leadership team. Lt Col Sushil Pradhan, a distinguished second generation officer, who had excelled in military career, passed Staff College in Competitive merit, been on UN mission in Africa and a trainer in Germany, joined the company in its early years and helped to build the famed "Information Services" business and is currently the COO and the backbone of the organisation. In the words of Pawan, "He had only two wishes when he joined in 2012. One that he wanted to stay in Pune and second that he wanted to do something related to research, reading and writing. We created an entire vertical for providing strategic insights on risk to global corporations. This vertical is now our flagship product and the future of MitKat."

MitKat is now organised into different operational verticals, which have their own peculiarities:

➤ Platform-based Information Services; includes threat intelligence, travel advisories and alerts. It has high visibility, great technology infusion, capable workforce and low-per-client revenues, decent margins and high-brand value

- ➢ Security Consulting & Design, a higher revenue and lower-margin business
- ➢ Cyber Security and Resilience, a rapidly growing business
- ➢ Integrity and Fraud Risk Management – the frauds are growing in complexity and future focus is on building digital forensic capabilities and tech-enabled fraud containment and detection measures
- ➢ Workforce Development offers a wide variety of customised training to global customers to include Women's Safety, Security Leadership, Crisis & Simulation exercises and Cyber Security training in partnership with Centre for Digital Transformation, a part of Confederation of Indian Industry
- ➢ Managed Services provides embedded security leaders who work to protect critical assets of the world's most respected organisations in consulting, technology, finance and manufacturing domains

Sam was the Founding CEO and saw MitKat stabilise, build, brand and foray overseas. After few years, Sam seamlessly handed over the baton to Pawan, the current CEO. While Sam as the Managing Director now handles Strategy, Business Development, Customer Relationship and Global Expansion, as the CEO, it is Pawan, where the buck stops finally. The CEO is responsible for keeping the company in good health and profitable, keeping clients happy and teams motivated.

Pawan is passionate about technology, and Sam and Pawan share the common view that MitKat by 2022 is going to be "asset light, data heavy and algorithmically inspired." MitKat leaders have already begun the process of digital transformation of the company. Sam said in a matter-of-fact manner, "We have to disrupt ourselves before we get disrupted."

The Founders of MitKat are already looking at new horizons with their future vision "To be world leaders in Information Services." They look at a two-fold path to realise this vision. Expand global reach by establishing permanent presence in USA and Europe and build a powerful platform to analyse huge amounts of data to provide actionable intelligence, while hiring fewer, albeit very capable, full-time employees coupled with on-call subject-matter experts of global stature.

Pawan says, "Let me try to explain it as simply as I can. The information and risk advisory services process knowledge by collection (data mining) → collation (data grading) → interpretation (data analytics) → storage and dissemination. As the data base increases, real time retrieval of data assumes critical importance. Introducing algorithm-based artificial intelligence (AI) platforms speeds up the entire process, enhances product quality and reduces dependency on human resources. Adding a predictive factor into data analytics upgrades the entire process to the next level of product quality. While the technology involved for the above is capital investment heavy, it makes business sense, as it reduces recurring expenditure on maintenance of human resources."

While MitKat has so far resisted the lure of external funding and focused instead on building a great organisation culture and solid foundations, now the Promoters seem favourably inclined to external funding to finance future expansion with a view to realising regional and leadership ambitions. "Investments in technology will continue to be pivotal to our growth," says Pawan.

The strength of the organisation lies in its connect with the environment and willingness to help start-ups and entrepreneurs. Pawan and Sam do spare their time for sharing experience with young entrepreneurs and advising veterans who transition to corporate careers.

MitKat has also made early-stage investments in a tech start up in the travel industry which is now doing very well.

Ideas on India

In 2013 with Maroof Raza as the Founder, Lt Gen Sudhir Sharma, Sam, Pawan and Parag have also been instrumental in creating a seminal thought leadership platform called "Ideas on India" which attracts some of the best speakers of the country at its events. The event highlights the constructive image of India to the world at large, India's world view and the world's perspective on India.

SAM SPEAKS

Learnings from the Army

"Selection and Maintenance of Aim" is the first principle of war. Army taught me the need to stay focused on the goal. There was great emphasis

on selection and maintenance of aim – selecting the correct objective, planning meticulously and executing flawlessly. Also the importance of reacting quickly and effectively to changing scenarios (agility). The Young Leaders of my generation always led from the front; they still do. Staying focused and doing less to do more has been a key element of MitKat's entrepreneurial journey. Despite the plethora of opportunities, distractions and roadblocks, we have stuck to our vision 'to be a leading global risk consultancy by 2025.'

A word about the military planning. I grew up in an old battalion, and even a mundane thing like dinner for guests is planned to the last T. The invitations go out a month or two in advance, it is personalised and acceptances and regrets are acknowledged with equal politeness. Who comes when, and is received how, is pre-decided. How many drinks are served; which course of dinner is candlelit and which one otherwise; which one with band and which one without; who is toasted and how; when does the National Anthem play; what happens post the dinner and how guests are seen off, as well as the post event activities – everything is planned to the last detail, and contingencies work out. The execution is nearly flawless. There is no hurrying or scurrying. Everything proceeds smoothly.

Much has been talked about the army's operational planning and why and how it consistently delivers in the face of adversity when everything else fails. The answer lies in the selection, training and grooming system. The army teaches to hire correct, train them well, plan meticulously and execute flawlessly. The importance of hiring correct and meticulous planning served me well in my entrepreneurial innings.

Early Days Were Challenging

The year was 2010 when we launched MitKat. The early entrepreneurial days were tough. We did not know how to form a company. No talent of any kind wanted to join us. Friends now viewed us as competition. No office fitted our budget. Cash was running out quickly. For the first time, I had begun to realise that without an Indian Army or a big corporate brand behind us, we were ordinary creatures in the big, bad outside world.

We ended up making losses and selling the only house that I had in the first year to ensure people got paid on time and no one was laid off, as we incurred learning costs and experienced the first non-payment.

In the second year, we did well and were able to recoup our losses.

Major Achievements

MitKat is seen as the thought leader in South Asia in Corporate Intelligence, Security & Risk Management. In the decade since its launch, MitKat has undertaken projects across 25 countries, with more than 50 of Top 100 global corporations. MitKat has a hi-tech AI-assisted Intel platform. MitKat's growth has been organic without external funding.

Building a great brand that continuously attracts, retains and retrains the best talent and a great organisational culture have been among MitKat's achievements, says one of the industry leaders.

Entrepreneurship is tough. Less than 10% achieve any modicum of success. You have to stay the course. Be goal-focused; do not lose hope. You are in the game, till you believe so.

Advice for the Mad Vets

Have a powerful idea. One that genuinely solves a big problem. Go in for a **platform-based model** rather than a traditional piped one.

There is **no right or wrong age to be an entrepreneur**. Steve Jobs, Bill Gates and Mark Zuckerberg started very early; the Founder of Kentucky Fried Chicken started post sixty. **Passion has no age.**

Do not be afraid of failure, though culturally in India it is easier said than done. We have failed more often than we have succeeded. Behind every two YESes has been eight NOs. If you have to fail, fail fast. Another way to look at it is – fail, fail, fail, until you succeed. After a failure, bounce back, hard and strong.

Focus: Do less to do more. Please do not do more than one thing at a time. I often hear wannabe entrepreneurs saying, "I am doing this and this and this, and at least one of them will succeed." I am ready to bet none will. We tried one thing and succeeded. Some of my friends tried three; they failed in all or at least two of these. If you do one thing that you truly believe in and are passionate about it, your chances of success increase.

People, people, people… Great co-founders and chemistry among them is most important. If you can surround yourself with people who believe in you and your idea, and not those who work only because they need a job or fat pay cheques, you will do well.

Staying on people, please surround yourself with people brighter and smarter than you. That's the best way to grow. Do not be insecure in their company.

Cash is king. Keep a close track of cash flows and collections. "Top line is vanity, bottom line is sanity, and cash is reality."

The rule of three: Whatever you plan will take three times more money, resources and time. So, kindly allow for more time, money and resources while planning.

Preparing for Entrepreneurship is like jumping from a 10 m swimming pool board. The more you think, the more you get scared. Aim and Fire or Fire and Aim! Well in our case, it was usually fire and aim?

Go with your gut. Do not have paralysis due to over analysis. Finally, there is no right or wrong choice. Whatever course you adopt or segment you choose, you have to make it work. If success is not coming, fail, but fail fast.

Your plan will not survive contact with the market. Yet planning is inevitable, and you must plan meticulously. Seek the advice of more experienced entrepreneurs. There are horses for courses. Do not go to chartered accountants to make a business plan. The plan must be yours.

A CA, CS or lawyer can help with company formation, accounting and compliance.

Pressure on entrepreneurs to succeed and scale up is intense; **please handle** it. Do not come under peer pressure.

An exciting option for Brigadiers and Generals to engage in nation building could be by angel funding and mentoring start-ups, after quickly re-orienting themselves and partnering with some veterans with corporate experience – their friends who left at 5 or 10 or 20 years' service and are now well settled into corporate or entrepreneurial careers. One of the ways forward would be a collaborative venture by five to ten Mad Vets with a capital investment of INR One Million each, build in an investment basket of total INR 1 Crore and provide angel investment and early-stage support to tech-enabled scalable start-ups in select domains. Or provide a pool of experts, which can be called upon for ambitious national projects or to beef up national capabilities during emergency situations and disasters.

Business Venture Options for Mad Vets

Business sense is an amalgamation of Skills, Passion and Market Understanding. Be prepared to unlearn, learn and relearn.

Be Agile. **Build an agile eco-system**. What is Amazon – is it a retailer or a tech giant? Amazon is a big eco-system! Apple is an entire eco-system! Uber is an eco-system. Build platform-based models which are scalable and link consumers and suppliers seamlessly.

Embrace Technology. Think disruptive, and grow exponentially. Do new things, and adopt new ways of doing things.

The biggest opportunities are coming at intersection of industries. Select an opportunity in sectors which are in early stage of growth cycle. High technology, platform-based business models provide good opportunities for success.

Philosophy Towards Life

'**Give more than you get**' and 'keep the other' while you converse or build relationships. '**Sound ethics makes great business sense**.'

Get the culture right, from the beginning. **Set the tone from the top**. There must be fair distribution of rewards and risks. We have been generous with sweat equity.

Be agile, adaptable and flexible. Keep reinventing yourself.

Personal Qualities

Qualities that have proved useful in my entrepreneurial journey:

➤ Focus
➤ Positive attitude
➤ Network and Eco-systems
➤ Resilience
➤ Ability to give more than you get

One Mantra for the Mad Vets who want to be Entrepreneurs

The mantra for success is not money, market conditions or team alone, though they have some part. It is the "WHY" that is very important. That is why the Wright Brothers succeeded in flying with literally no funding, supported by a team with no formal degrees, but with a missionary zeal to change the world, while a legend named Samuel Pierpont Langley, with a top-class team, funding and government and media support struggled and finally quit flying the day the Wright Brothers succeeded.

Entrepreneurship involves a fundamental mismatch between resource and ambition. It must have a value and purpose beyond making you rich and famous. It must pursue **a cause that attracts other talented, capable professionals.**

So select your aim, maintain your aim, and stay the course.

Views on Future of India

Research indicates that from 3500 BC to 1700 AD, Indian GDP was nearly a quarter of the world's and India was one of the top two global powers. The digital revolution, the flattening of the world and the demographic dividend provides us great opportunity to reclaim our lost glory.

Our time has come. I have great faith in the young generation and their ability to reclaim India's lost glory. The Indian diaspora is already excelling across the world. Once we have enabling eco-systems, they will excel here and we will once again become *"Sone ki Chidiya."*

Willingness to Mentor Mad Vets

We would be more than happy to mentor Mad Vets. In fact, we are already mentoring a dozen of Mad Vets. We are also engaged in readying veterans for a second career by running Veterans Transformation Programs and supporting other such initiatives like "Soldier2ndLife" and "Forces Network." There have been notable success stories, of course, along with some disappointments.

The Role of Spouse

When Vineeta and I got married, like other army spouses, she was charmed by the army and its unique way of life. Army spouses understand the concept that service to the nation takes precedence over family commitments. Family has a defining role in our lives. The sacrifices made by army spouses often go unsung. Vineeta has made sacrifices to ensure that I was able to perform my duties to the Nation; she holds the family together, yet finds time for social causes. She has had a great role in bringing up the children and giving them the correct 'sanskaar.'

We were expecting our first child while I was working with the Missile Program. I had even foregone the first mandatory chance to appear for the prestigious Defence Services Staff Course qualifying examination, so that we could be together during the special time that our first child would be born. Just prior to the delivery time, I received information about my boss' inability to make it for the test firing of a missile, an event of national importance. It was the call of duty. I just had adequate time to drop her at the maternity hospital along with my mother-in-law, before taking off on a long drive to the Interim Test Range Facility, 500 km away, driving through the night, but making it on time.

Again during a long operational deployment, Vineeta had to fend for herself with two small children while I was a Combat Team Commander for impending operations on the Western borders. This led her to master her driving skills a little better. We have developed a healthy and mutual respect for each other and follow a policy of non-interference in professional and social affairs. Of course, on family matters, her decision is final.

One time when we had slight difference of opinion was when the time came for me to share my thoughts on leaving the army. She eventually concurred, albeit a bit reluctantly, after reminding me, "I married the Army."

Vineeta is a fantastic homemaker, a former teacher of repute and now a social worker. We have always lived a very frugal lifestyle. While I am busy with my entrepreneurial venture, Vineeta now devotes her time as a social service volunteer and is associated with the Brahm Kumari Organisation, counselling those in distress and helping the needy.

PAWAN SPEAKS

Learnings from the Navy

As a young officer in the Navy, you are a jack of all trades. I broke silos by pushing my subordinates into additional responsibilities in lateral disciplines.

As a submariner you learn to maximise your resources; there's no choice. So I developed the trait of making do with constraints. It bodes well for the economy of the company.

Being under life-threatening stress for days on end, the submariners tend to develop a nose for trouble. This sixth sense helped me in seeing problem areas early on, enabling reaction time to handle difficult issues.

Difficulties

Our first big break also proved to be our most difficult hour. We were awarded the contract to provide e-security arrangements for international and national VIPs during a sporting event involving multiple pan-India locations. We overnight hired two officers and twenty-two ex-servicemen and immediately imported a self-propelled full vehicle scanner for the task. Adequate time was not available to procure the licence needed for its road movement. With fixtures at multiple locations, it was a herculean effort to plan and execute the logistics of its transportation on trailer. To make matters worse, the event got involved in legal controversy whereby our contract was adversely impacted, resulting in non-payment of our dues. As a matter of principle, we did not dehire the ex-servicemen and retained them on our rolls till we could ensure their resettlement elsewhere. I had to go without salary for almost six months with no alternate income, unlike most of the veterans have, and Sam had to sell his house to meet the dues.

Three Major Achievements

We are a brand to reckon with in the global arena in our domain of operations.

Being a technology-centric company makes us the most sought-after platform provider.

HR empowerment has been our biggest achievement. We have supremely talented and capable colleagues, who are with us out of choice and not because they do not have an alternative. They display great sense of ownership, loyalty to the organisation – almost everyone who has left still remains in touch, a trait common in armed forces, but missing in the business world which tends to be more transactional – and are committed to excellence. Our senior/gen-next leadership has been with us for five to eight years.

We have consciously invested heavily in HR and hired people who are better than us. This gives us space for thought and planning for the future.

Advice for the Mad Vets

First of all, there can be no half-hearted effort, or it would be tantamount to losing the match even before the effort has begun. It's OK to say OK to hardship, but there will be times when there will be no profit, so no income. Will you be OK with indeterminate income, and even more important, will your family be OK with this concept?

The "why" of the venture is more important than the how, and then your business strategy should be aligned to your why. Also, the why, what and how of today may not be the why, what and how of tomorrow. So be prepared for periodic reviews and mid-course corrections.

Don't go it alone, take partners. A partner's value is realised during hard times. Choose your business partner very, very wisely, with the same rigour as choosing a life partner.

Business Venture Options for Mad Vets

For me the Veterans generally fall into two broad categories, the Opinionated and the Adaptable.

For the Opinionated, I would recommend self-driven ventures such as investments in finance, advisory fields and even non-team assignments.

Manpower-intensive, E-commerce and Technology start-ups would be ideal for the Adaptable ones.

Philosophy Towards Life

I have learnt by seeing my father engaged in his manufacturing business that no job is small and you are your own best seller. Hands-on work is the best for a new venture.

One must give back to society. I see a vast gap between Academia and Industry. An overwhelming number of graduates are just not industry ready. One way to close this gap is by Industry professionals doubling as part-time or even guest faculty to educate the students about the industry skills needed to be a success. Sam, Sushil and I along with our other colleagues have worked hard to build a relationship with the industry and take out time to visit and share knowledge and experience with students. We at MitKat also spend a fair amount of time with our interns.

For the past five years, I have been associated with Narsi Monjee Institute of Management Studies as an Associate Professor in Digital Platforms to teach Information Technology. I have been a visiting faculty at Symbiosis Centre for Information Technology and was on their Board of Studies for a few years.

Personal Qualities

Humility and empathy are very important. Give more than you get. Listen more than you speak.

Be a lifelong learner. You can learn from everyone.

Balance is important. Live life well. Do not put off living.

Be adaptable and useful first. Please shed the attitude of entitlement, and see the growth happen.

One Mantra for the Mad Vets

Improve listening skills. There is a misconception that Veterans are good listeners. In my experience, they are really bad at it. This is one skill which if we learn, the success is guaranteed. We are used to listening very hierarchically. In today's VUCA world we need to listen 360 degrees. You never know; the game-changing suggestion might come from most unexpected quarters.

Views on Future of India

The future of India is very bright and full of immense possibilities. We are well poised to become an advanced country and a global power in our lifetime.

The Small and Medium Enterprises are currently forming the backbone of our industrial economy. They have to upscale to take advantage of our national demographic dividend. I foresee a bright future for mergers and consolidation in our economy.

Willingness to Mentor Mad Vets

Yes, and why not. In fact, for the right startup venture, I could even think of turning into an Angel Investor. I will be happy to share the mistakes I have done and help them in not repeating the same in addition to some valuable advice also.

Role of Spouse

Noopur has been the anchor in the rollercoaster ride of my life. Always supportive, an excellent human being and always challenging me to achieve greater heights.

When I was in seventh standard in school, during the community gathering on Independence Day, I was tasked to speak on 'My India.' When I came onto the dais, I just froze and couldn't speak, and rushed out in tears. This phobia of public speaking was ever present within me, even after I had joined the Navy. Noopur understood this weakness of mine and took it upon herself to get me to overcome this fear. With her active assistance I have been able to convert the weakness into my forte.

She is intelligent, creative and highly articulate. Despite qualifying as an MBA, she voluntarily forsook her career, to put her family first. She is an excellent writer and currently in the process of authoring a book named *I met God at the Cafe.*

Even Sam acknowledges her strength and wisdom. So he first approached her about the idea of floating our own business concern and leveraged her support to convince me.

* * *

The power of thought described

THE POWER OF I

Genesis
The power of I (self) flows from three fountains:
➤ Fountain of Understanding (of self)
➤ Fountain of Freedom (of individual choice)
➤ Fountain of Responsibility (of reaping consequences)

Power of Choice

I have inherent power to understand true self,
And in so doing understand nature itself.

I am unique and can neither be recreated nor destroyed;
I do change form to flit from dimension to dimension.

I have the power of choice;
To exercise or abdicate this power is my choice.

I have the power of emotion;
To be led by emotions or rule the emotions is my life.

I have the power to access eternal knowledge;
To apply or not is how future I decide.

I have the power to succumb or reject pain and pleasure;
To progress or retard journey on the chosen path.

To nurture my environment or inflict damage colossal,
I have the power to command.

I have the power of thought to be what I think;
Pauper or king, scholar or soldier is for me to define.

I have the power to be strong to turn the tide
Or vacillate on action to permit events to sweep me aside.

I can never be put down, as I have the power to rebound;
I can move mountains; such is the power of faith at my command.

I have the power to stretch my desires or forego infinite wants
And be satisfied with the minutest of trivia.

I have the power to anchor to rock of principles
Or be swayed in directions by gentle breezes.

I have the power to fly straight as an arrow to the chosen mark
Or meander meaninglessly on a destination-less journey.

I have responsibility of the power I exercise
And power of understanding the consequences of my choice.

I have the power to accept, my verbal aloud aside,
That my past present and future I and only I decide.
I am, I know, I do, I accept.

- Col RS Sidhu

* * *

Innovative Trust Based Lease Contract Farming Entrepreneur

All ventures where trust is the key factor with the customer should be the natural first choice business options for the Veterans.

- Lt Col Subhash Deswal

Twice presented with the "Most Innovative Farmer" award by the Government of Uttar Pradesh, recognised with a Fellowship by the Indian Council for Agriculture Research in 2019 and invitee to the World Carrot Congress held in USA and Poland, Lt Col Subhash Deswal is one of the most recognised Mad Vets in the farming segment of West Uttar Pradesh.

Subhash was born in a family of four brothers and a sister, in District Jhajjar, Haryana. A few years into schooling at Bahadurgarh, his elder brother was martyred while serving with 4 JAT in the Fazilka sector, during the 1971 war against Pakistan. It was a strong desire of their father that one son should be in service of the nation in the army. To fulfil the desire of their father, Subhash appeared for the entrance examination of Sainik School Kunjpura and secured admission to the school in 1972. The same year he also qualified in the examination for the Haryana Government Education Scholarship.

An avid reader of daily newspapers, he became fascinated with the work of the famous Supreme Court constitutional lawyer Nani Palkhiwala. The fascination soon developed into hero worship, and he began dreaming of a career in law. Subhash became disinterested in joining the army. As a result, he could not qualify in the first attempt for the entrance examination to NDA. In 1979, just before the second attempt to qualify for NDA, he sustained a fracture in his leg. Using this as a justifiable excuse, he secured an exemption from the school principal to withdraw from the NDA entrance examination and returned home.

Army Life

His parents were stunned and refused to talk to him. His mother even threatened to jump into a well. Subhash was so moved by the strong desire of his parents that he immediately travelled from Bahadurgarh to Patiala, despite his medical condition, to appear in the entrance examination. He went on to qualify the entrance examination and joined NDA.

After successfully passing out from NDA, and subsequently IMA, he was commissioned into 12th Battalion of the Mechanised Infantry Regiment. Raised as 8 PARA and subsequently converted to 16 MAHAR, it proudly carries its designation of 12 MECH INF (8 PARA-16 MAHAR). The unit maintained its PARACHUTE tradition by providing Infantry Combat Vehicle component to the PARACHUTE BRIGADE. The battalion at the time was one of the most versatile units of the Indian Army, tasked as it was to maintain a Mechanised Infantry Company in airborne role and also trained for offensive operations in riverine terrain. True to the traditions of the Paltan, Subhash volunteered for Para jumps and earned the coveted Parachute Wings. Very early in his army career, he learnt to live his dreams. Uncertainties of life no longer awed him.

Though Subhash was not aware of it then, 1986 would prove to be a watershed year in his life. His army unit was stationed in Kapurthala, a small town in Punjab. The Officer Mess of the unit was located next to the yard of a Sikh land developer with a fleet of dozen odd tractors and trolleys. As a young officer, while enjoying his morning cup of tea after physical training, Subhash became fascinated by the daily sight of all these tractors being marshalled out in convoy with military precision one after the other on landscaping task. A yearning took root in his subconscious to be the proud owner of a similar fleet. Little did he know that it would take him two decades to successfully convert this yearning into reality.

While in command of a Mechanised Infantry Company, he had the opportunity to be deployed in counter-insurgency role. During this deployment he learnt the intricacies of boundary management, intelligence gathering, detailed and innovative planning and meticulous conduct of operations. This experience would prove to be invaluable in his life as an entrepreneur.

During army life he developed a reputation for hard work, an eye for detail and out-of-the-box thinking, qualities that would hold him in good stead in his second career. Ethical practices and behaviour became second nature to him. He also developed a distinct dislike for being taken advantage of.

Changing the Uniform

During this time, one of his brothers shifted base to Sikandrabad, in Bulandshahar District of Uttar Pradesh and established a petroleum fuel filling station. Subhash would often visit Sikandrabad during leave and developed a friend circle. One of them, Lal Krishan Yadav, became really close to him. He had completed his Masters in Chemistry and was running a pesticide and chemicals business. Lal Krishan was dissatisfied with the small scale of his business and would often express a desire to enter into a major business venture in partnership with Subhash, once the latter came out from the army.

By the year 2000 AD, Subhash came to the conclusion that to realise his life aims he would have to leave the army. This was around the time that he was posted in New Delhi. One afternoon, while enjoying a glass of beer with his dear friend Col Ranjit Deswal from Brigade of The Guards, he announced his intention to leave the army and sought his advice.

Ranjit was quite blunt. In his assessment, Subhash was not cut out for life outside the army owing to his tendency to question "unfair trade practices" and also lacking life skills to handle government regulators! Notwithstanding, he recommended farm sector as the best bet for Subhash, as it had minimum government regulation and interference.

Subhash immediately spoke over phone to his friend Lal Krishan to commence preparatory planning for starting an agricultural business. He also insisted that the business would be in compliance with government regulations. Despite reservations from Lal Krishan, Subhash insisted that in the long run it was advantageous to establish a reputation for ethical practices and behaviour. The name and reputation of an army officer carried a certain weight with the customers at large as well as government officials and needed to be leveraged to own advantage. This policy was to be sacrosanct and the cornerstone of their corporate actions.

Subhash, as was his wont, got down to learning the nitty gritty of farm practices. He ignored the conventional wisdom of there being no profits in agriculture. In his assessment, the overwhelming majority of farmers conducted farm operations unprofessionally. They lacked discipline, hence were irregular in providing farm inputs to crops. Reactions were slow to counter fast-changing situations created by crop infections and weather unpredictability. They were content with traditional cropping methods, even when the desired dividends were not being achieved. The big farmers rarely spent more than an hour onsite on the fields. Government policies of control over farm inputs and staple farm produce prices tilted the scale heavily in favour of the traders. There was no willingness to experiment beyond traditional crops to get around inefficient government farming sector policies. Subhash was convinced that bringing in military skills of SWOT analysis, leadership traits and detailed planning, including contingencies would enable them to overcome the assessed inefficiencies. In the army there is no prize for runners up; hence, failure was not an option.

Sikandrabad, though a crime-prone area, had certain advantages. It was close to Delhi. Subhash's brother and Lal Krishan, the chosen partner, were well established in the area. Land was available at comparatively cheap rates, and labour was easily available.

Leave and weekends were spent in discussions and assessments. After preliminary surveys, infrastructure planning and assessing finance requirements, it was felt that the best way forward would be to gain first-hand experience. It was decided that the first year shall be utilised to undertake trial farming of four products, that is, potato, onion, okra (ladies finger) and carrot. The year was 2003.

Contract Farming Entrepreneur

The next three years were spent in trial and learning. By 2006, Subhash was confident that they were ready. He left the army the same year and plunged head on into farming. Their operations were based on two innovative thoughts. First, they hired land on contract lease rather than making heavy capital investments to purchase land. Second, they selected Carrot Nantes (pale orange colour carrot) crop, a farm produce of South India, for commercial farming, whereas only red-coloured carrot was produced in North India. Carrot was not produced in the general area of Secunderabad.

The name selected for their venture was Sunshine Farm. Subhash started handling marketing, future planning, technical equipment and liaison. Lal Krishan handled production, production associates and service providers. Production soon became their strong point owing to the diligence and dynamism of Lal Krishan in the fields.

The unethical practices rampant in the wholesale market confronted the nascent business with their first challenge. The traders time and again underpaid the contracted rate of the carrots under some pretext or the other. The choice was to accept the unfair trade practices or do something. Subhash was not one to take the situation lying down. After a lot of brainstorming, the duo adopted the strategy to grow big, improve quality and establish round-the-year presence in the market.

This set them on the course of the next set of innovations.

To grow big, they invited selected farmers to become their produce associates. The produce associates were provided with farm inputs such as quality seeds, approved fertilisers, pesticides, herbicides and agriculture support services such as washing, grading and storage. Thus, with a minimum of investment, their acreage under cultivation multiplied phenomenally. The production of carrots crossed the tipping point, enabling them to favourably influence wholesale trading rates.

The second leg of the strategy was to develop service providers by providing short-term financial support against assessed future crop produce value. The agriculture service providers now became the owners of mechanical farm equipment. Sunshine Farm was relieved of the heavy load of daily repair and maintenance of technical equipment. As specialisation increased so did the quality of produce. Subhash took on the task of developing and modifying equipment to replace or minimise employment of manual labour in the entire production chain. Within a decade, they developed the largest mutually supportive, interdependent and self- sustaining farm eco-system in Uttar Pradesh, comprising more than hundred produce associates and service providers. As Sunshine Farm grew so did their associates and so did their economic and social status. They had become big enough to have decisive influence in the wholesale market as also in the government.

Taking up the third leg of their challenge to establish round-the-year presence in the market almost proved to be their undoing. To hold the produce, it had to be preserved. The existing cold storages were all oriented to preserve potatoes. Storing carrots in these cold stores resulted in huge wastages. They hired consultants to develop cold storage facilities for carrot. After taking a bank loan, they constructed a cold storage for carrots, but it was unsuccessful to fully preserve the carrots for prolonged duration. This was an existential crisis for the Sunshine Farm.

But Subhash did not lose heart. He first sold off all his properties and then raised money from close family to ensure payment. He ensured there was no default to banks, and payment to associates were made as per schedule. This policy at the peak of their most severe crisis established their reputation of reliability in the market. The losses were recouped in the next two harvesting seasons owing to the strength of their production capability.

After recovering from the crisis, Subhash and Lal Krishan were now ready to move to the next level. Sunshine Farm was renamed as Sunshine Vegetables Private Limited and an Integrated Rural Agriculture Hub was established. The concept incorporates the entire cycle from in-house procurement of seeds and farm inputs, cultivation, harvesting, processing, storage, marketing and transportation to customer. He built the first carrot storage in India, which was a failure. The second time around, he relentlessly worked to gather expert knowledge on storage of carrots and built the first successful carrot cold storage in India.

The future of Sunshine Vegetables Private Limited looks bright. In addition to carrots, peas and corn are also being added to the basket of their produce. A carrot-ready cold storage is fully functional. The work for the construction of the processing plant with Individually Quick Frozen (IQF) technology, pack house and distribution centre with multiple cold storages have been planned for the next year.

SUBHASH SPEAKS

Major Achievements

Small land holdings are the bane of the Indian agriculture sector. Poor literacy, social dogmas and generations-old deep-rooted fear of legal documents are an impediment to land consolidation. So consolidating land to make it a financially viable entity, based on trust alone, is our biggest success.

Small farmers are routinely exploited by farm input providers both in terms of price and quality. By centrally negotiating with the input providers on behalf of all our farm lessee contractors, we created an economics of scale whereby we ensure quality and cost control of all farm inputs. This has enhanced profit margins for us as well as the small farmers.

The small farmers have no capacity to hold their produce for better returns. This places them at the mercy of the trader. Again, by engaging in economics of scale and quality control, we introduced the concept of pre-sale of farm produce even prior to sowing the crop. Today, 60% to 70% of our produce associates' crop is contracted to be sold prior to sowing. This has minimised the role of traditional farm produce traders, thereby ensuring higher price for the remainder of the produce.

We are undoubtedly the single largest producer of English carrots in India. Our effort has had a beneficial impact on the economy and lives of the people in and around the small town of Sikandrabad, which has now been dubbed as the 'Carrot Capital of India' by *Frontline*, a reputed national magazine. Many enterprising people in the city have built their business based on the innovations in the farm mechanisation model spearheaded by us.

Advice for the Mad Vets

There are three major impediments to entrepreneurship by the Veterans. First is the deep-rooted averseness to undertake financial risk. Right from the time of joining the service it is ingrained into them to avoid financial risks. It is a no brainer that there is no entrepreneurship without risk acceptance.

Secondly, the know-all attitude needs to be discarded. There should be no hesitation in meticulously acquiring knowledge of your new profession.

Thirdly, in overwhelming instances of Veteran couples who come to me for advice on a second career, I notice a distinct lack of support from the spouse in following the entrepreneur route to the second career. The Veteran's spouses simply do not have faith in their entrepreneurial skills. It virtually sounds the death knell to any entrepreneurial pretensions of the Veteran.

On the other hand is the case of Ex Daffedar Harender Singh of 70 Armoured Regiment, who served in the army for 16 years from 1992 to 2009. He joined us in 2012 as a produce associate with 20 bighas of land. Today he crops 900 bighas land on contract lease, producing 4500 metric tonnes of carrots and supplies as far as Amritsar in Punjab, Bajpur in Uttar Pradesh and Bhopal in Madhya Pradesh. In addition, he is also engaged in property development, wherein he initially invested 5% shares in property development of established businesses. Today, the investment ratio is in reverse.

Options for the Mad Vets to Undertake New Ventures

All ventures where trust is the key factor with the customer should be the natural first choice business options for the Veterans. There is an acute dearth of professionalism, reliability and quality in the property dealing and service provider industry segment.

In the farm sector, there is virtually no competition for the professionals, even new-entrant professionals. Ever-increasing population ensures no major challenges in marketing the produce. Overwhelming majority of tillers of soil continue to follow traditional and outdated farming practices and are void of discipline in ensuring timely inputs. With enhanced customer awareness, traceability of the farm product is gaining increasing significance in marketing of the produce. The inherent discipline of the Veterans gives them a headstart in systematic planning, eye for detail and recording of crop data all vital to establish traceability of the farm product.

Philosophy Towards Life

Anchoring self to ethical standards simplifies personal and business life and provides immense returns.

Personal Qualities that Have Helped You

The three Ps of punctuality, probity and perseverance are the cornerstone of my life. The fourth P of procrastination is a strict No-No as a leader.

The Future of India

The Indian industry at production level is vibrant. The new-age professionals are not willing to settle for second position. The attitude of bureaucracy too is changing for the good. Fresh breath of air is visible in the next-gen politicians. All these are signs which bode well for the country.

One Mantra for the Mad Vets

We are first learners and then an entrepreneur. The start point has to be: "I know nothing." We have to immerse ourselves into learning the chosen subject from scratch and then plan market entry.

Willingness to Mentor Mad Vets

Yes. The possibilities for future growth in my field are immense. As we aspire to expand into new verticals, the only resource which is cramping my lateral expanse is experienced produce associates with fire in their bellies. The Mad Vets who are willing to take up the challenge shall always be welcome.

On Role of Spouse

Sunita is a very efficient homemaker. Her experience as an army spouse has made her independent and practical. She understands that my profession would always take precedence over discharge of family responsibilities.

So when the time came for me to take a call on leaving the army to start second innings as an entrepreneur, she was very supportive of the idea. But her support came with a caveat.

Being a practical individual, she said that our children's future should not be put at stake by the vagaries of the entrepreneur world. So she stated in a matter-of-fact conversation that my pension and rental from the residential property would be hers to use. I conceded to her request.

She has supported my business venture through thick and thin. Her forte is managing our vast array of family and social relationships, thereby ensuring my full attention to my profession.

✳ ✳ ✳

International Consultant For Infrastructure Development

The basic building block of my learning from the armed forces is sincerity of purpose. From sincerity flows hard work, which in turn necessitates physical fitness and mental robustness. In the business world, the requirement of mental robustness is more important.

- Lt Col NPS Bana

Lt Col Naresh Pal Singh Bana, post release from the army, wears six different hats in varied fields:

➤ International consultant in the field of infrastructure development as Founder and Managing Director, BBV Consultant LLP (Limited Liability Partnership), incorporated in March 2011

➤ Specialist in post-disaster reconstruction as Founder and Managing Director, Astainable Construction Pvt. Ltd., incorporated in October 2016

➤ Providing app-based veterinary care connect to cattle owners in West Uttar Pradesh as Founder and Managing Director, Gajanan Innovations Pvt. Ltd., incorporated in November 2018

➤ Treasurer and Chairman, Editorial Board, World Association of Public Private Partnership (PPP) Units and Professionals, Geneva, Switzerland, an organisation engaged in capacity building and knowledge sharing in PPP domain

➢ Executive Vice Chairman, Indo-Sri Lanka Chamber of Commerce & Industry, engaged in investor guidance and trade facilitation between the two countries

➢ Engaged in ITES Skill Development and Social Support as Vice Chairman, Jan Kalyan Samvaad Foundation, a not-for-profit company, established in February 2015

In just under a decade, Naresh has undertaken international consultancies and infrastructure projects with United Nations Economic Commission for Europe (UNECE), France, Oman, Sri Lanka, Zimbabwe, Nepal and Myanmar, and one-off trading assignments in Namibia and Tanzania. The cumulative annual turnover of the various companies being run by him is modest, but the influence and impact of his entrepreneurship goes much beyond that.

Naresh Bana, as Managing Director of BBV Consultants LLP, is a Team Leader at UNECE, Geneva. His team drafted Standard for PPP in Railways, which was released in November 2018. He has been commended for his efforts by UNECE in 2018.

Astainable Construction Pvt. Ltd., under his leadership, is privileged to have been commended in 2018 by the Ambassador of Sultanate of Oman to India for undertaking post-earthquake housing reconstruction project in Nepal in difficult hilly terrain.

Early Life

Naresh, born in the year 1964, was the youngest of five siblings. He did his early schooling at Lucknow and Meerut, the places of posting of his father who worked with the Uttar Pradesh Cooperative Societies.

By the time Naresh completed his sixth standard, his father retired, and the family returned to their native village Chitauli, near Hapur, a mofussil town in West Uttar Pradesh. The village had no phone, newspapers or television, modern trappings taken for granted in today's world. Life was tough but simple. It was as if time itself was at a standstill. The nearest school was in Hapur, roughly five kilometres from the village, and the route from the village to the school was along a dirt footpath, crossed by a seasonal stream. During monsoons, the villagers would keep bundles of maize stalks at the crossing place for use as ad hoc floating pontoon for pedestrian traffic. Naresh recalls, "While studying in Class VII, once I fell off the maize-stalk bundle into the stream during monsoons. My fellow schoolmates helped me out of the waters. Fortunately, I was able to hold my schoolbag above my head, thus ensuring that my books remained dry. We then ran the rest of the distance to school so that our clothes could dry up." For the next six years, Naresh walked or cycled ten kilometres daily to attend school.

Naresh remembers with pride a civil engineering project that he informally supervised during 1980 while studying in eleventh standard. It so happened that his father was constructing a house in the village. But cement at that time was a controlled commodity. The BDO proposed installing a biogas project on their land and offered controlled cement bags alongside. The biogas plant was to be constructed using a new design, which has a concrete dome and not the conventional steel dome. The BDO was unable to explain the engineering drawing to the contractor. Naresh, who was around, offered to explain the drawings to the mason. The offer was a godsend for the BDO, and he readily accepted. Naresh became the defacto engineer-in-charge of the construction of the first biogas plant in the entire development block. Naresh could not have imagined that three decades down the line, he would be incorporating his own construction firm.

In 1981, Naresh joined Meerut College as an undergraduate and moved to the college hostel. However, he was uncomfortable with the lackadaisical attitude of a large number of hostel students. So he approached his brother-in-law, a PhD scholar in the same college, to arrange his stay with him in the PhD scholars' hostel. There Naresh came in regular touch with some illustrious scholars who would go on to be reputed entrepreneurs, politicians and lawyers in their own right.

Being in the company of bright scholars, Naresh got motivated to prepare for civil services examinations. Then one of his classmates advised Naresh to appear for Combined Defence Services examination. Naresh accepted the advice and cleared his written examinations and the ensuing Services Selection Board interview process.

Life in the Army

On 02 August 1984, Naresh joined training as a Gentleman Cadet IMA, Dehradun. He was the first person from Bana clan to do so.

Unfortunately, during his second term of training in IMA, Naresh sustained a serious fracture of his tibia and fibula bones in his right leg while running for Battle Physical Efficiency Test. He was evacuated to MH and taken straight to the operation theatre. At the MH, the medical staff queried him whether his stomach was empty. On getting a negative response they decided to operate upon his fractured leg without any anaesthesia. Two burly nursing assistants were detailed to hold him down on the operating table while the orthopaedic surgeon started reduction of the fractured bones. However, the pain was so unbearable that Naresh hurled the two nursing assistants away from his body. The operation was thereafter conducted under local anaesthesia.

After eight weeks the hospital authorities realised that the bones had become misaligned while healing. Naresh was diagnosed as unfit for army service and referred to Command Hospital at Lucknow for further treatment and medical discharge from service. There Naresh found himself in company of two more Gentleman Cadets, interestingly enough, also with fractures in their right legs.

Naresh narrates an interesting incident of his stay in the Command Hospital. "Out of boredom, the three of us Gentleman Cadets, bed patients, decided to go on an escapade to Hazratganj to watch the movie, *Umrao Jaan*. We arranged for three cycle rickshaws, through a helpful civilian conservancy employee. It was mid-afternoon, in peak of summer, and the corridors and open premises were deserted. We were surreptitiously moved by wheelchairs to the cycle rickshaws, waiting at the isolated cut in the perimeter wall at the rear side of the hospital. The cavalcade of three cycle rickshaws carrying a single person each, crew cut hair, dressed in white shorts, white T-shirts, white PT shoe on one foot and white plaster on right leg held extended and resting on the rickshaw pullers seat in front was a sight to behold on the fashionable Hazratganj Avenue. On arrival at the movie hall, we came to know that the tickets were sold out, and the movie show had commenced. Determinedly, we asked for the manager of the hall. The manager presented himself instantly and deputed two staff each to help us climb the stairs to the balcony. He had three additional chairs placed for us to watch the movie and honoured us even more by restarting the movie afresh.

In the interim, the warden of the Officers Ward was at his wits end wondering how he could explain three-bed ridden patients absenting themselves from the Officers Ward without anyone becoming aware. So when we returned equally discretely, the distraught warden was highly relieved, and, after using some choicest four-letter words to let off his steam, decided against reporting the matter."

To the good fortune of Naresh, the orthopaedic specialist decided to again operate on his fracture, and it healed successfully post second surgery. By the end of the year, Naresh was declared fit for military duty, rejoined training at IMA and passed out as a commissioned officer into the Corps of Engineers in June 1986. He was allotted 65 ENGINEERS, a highly specialised bridging unit designed to provide assault bridging for offensive operations by the Strike Corps of the IA.

Within a month of his commissioning, Naresh proceeded to CME at Pune for a six-month Young Officer's Course. In his continuous quest to make himself physically fitter, Naresh joined the Sailing and Rowing Club at CME. Then Major PK Uberoi, an Arjuna Award winner, was in-charge of the club. He noticed the latent talent in Naresh and advised him to concentrate on rowing. Naresh developed a passion for rowing and soon represented CME in Maharashtra State Regatta, winning a gold medal in his team event. He followed it up by winning a silver medal in his team event at the National Championships held in January 1988 and was selected for the training camp for the Indian team for Asiad 1990.

Unfortunately, his Young Officer's Course was over, and he had to urgently report back to his regiment. Operation Meghdoot was underway in Siachen Glacier, Operation Pawan was in full swing in Sri Lanka, and tensions were also brewing along the Western and Northern borders. Owing to impending operational commitments, the unit could not spare him for attending the National Rowing Camp. Naresh now turned his attention, with equal passion, to master the technical and operational aspects of the bridging equipment held by his unit. His proficiency was acknowledged. Technological innovations and problem solving became his forte. This was also the time when he got married to Sandhya in May 1989.

The period 1990 to 1993 was spent by Naresh completing his three-year degree course from CME, Pune. Sandhya and Naresh were blessed with their first child during this period.

Naresh also continued to pursue his first love, reading. This pursuit led him to secure a postgraduate degree in Military Studies from Meerut University in 1995, Master of Science degree in Defence & Strategic Studies from Madras University in 2000, MBA degree from IGNOU in 2003 and Construction Management degree from reputed National Institute of Construction Management & Research in Delhi in 2005. In 2010, Naresh attended an Executive Management course titled "Strategic Financing for Small Business" from Harvard Business School, USA. Currently, too, Naresh is following his passion by pursuing management from Noida International University.

The uniqueness of Naresh lies in not only his quest for theoretical knowledge, but also excelling in the practical and innovative application of the knowledge thus acquired. In the year 2002, he designed and implemented an online official correspondence management system at Brigade Headquarters while functioning as Brigade Major.

It was as AQMG of a Mountain Division responsible for logistics and infrastructure management that his technical innovation skills came to the forefront. In the mountains, availability of water is a major factor impacting the course of military operations. Naresh undertook a study and innovated a unique water storage strategy wherein using two element-impervious polymer coating water would be retained in shallow ponds over hills. The technical paper of this innovation was published in *Sapper Journal* published by CME, Pune in 2004. Naresh was also privileged to present this innovation at Seattle University, USA in November 2005.

In 2004, Naresh interacted with National Mission for Bamboo Application, under Department of Science & Technology, for various bamboo-based innovations. As acknowledgement of his effort, one of the sustainable structures was named 'Bana Hut.'

In May 2005, he received intimation of not getting empanelled for promotion to next rank. Naresh had reached the pinnacle of his active service in the army. He was then not aware that this disappointment would be the precursor to the most exciting phase of his service career and the turning point in his life.

IRCON, a Public Sector Unit under Ministry of Railways, was in the process of constructing Udhampur Srinagar Baramulla Rail Line, a project of far-reaching geostrategic impact even beyond national borders. It was being executed in the most difficult terrain for construction of railways infrastructure, and the adverse security situation in the region further compounded the difficulties in project execution. Under the circumstances, the Ministry of Railways approached the Army Headquarters for posting suitable army officers to supervise the project on ground.

Naresh was shortlisted and offered posting on deputation as Joint General Manager, IRCON, owing to his technical expertise and dynamic image of being a "go getter." He accepted the offer and joined the project in Kashmir Valley in the beginning of 2006.

The situation on the ground was grim when Naresh joined the project. Only 50% of the Valley Railway work had been executed, and the deadline was 2007. Work on the project was virtually stalled owing to frequent terrorist attacks on the project engineers. He also sensed a distinct lack of enthusiasm in the local IRCON team about the placement of an army officer to manage the project on the ground.

As he took stock of the situation, Naresh realised that the situation needed initiative and activism beyond the scope of specified working norms. To create an enabling environment for work to proceed unhindered, there was a need to manage state entities, opaque non-state groups and influencers, and own teams with their own unique dynamics. Rule books were both facilitators and a hindrance. Dynamic leadership was the need of the hour. Naresh enforced strict work ethics and discipline by leading from the front.

Engineers started regular site supervision. Advance planning and coordination became the norm to foresee contingencies, and plans were put in place to overcome work hazards and difficulties. Whether it was the response to the killing of the Personal Security Officer of an Engineer, terrorists barging into the residential quarters of the staff, evacuation of 200-odd engineers in the face of anti-outsider agitation by misguided youth, ensuring the setting up of infrastructure for CRPF camp at Naina Butpora, which was frequently destroyed by the terrorists, or handling the request to surrender a dreaded terrorist, Naresh was always at the forefront to handle the situation.

He soon established a reputation as the "Go-to Man" for any coordination between the State administration and Kashmir Rail project, empowering him with influence beyond the scope of his role. All visits of international delegations, diplomats and government functionaries were managed by him. The contacts established by Naresh during this period would prove to be of immense value in his subsequent entrepreneur life.

Naresh employed his army experience for managing external environment by undertaking social welfare impact works such as repairs to mosques and burial grounds in the area and constructing a cremation ground. As most of his staff were Muslims, he undertook full Ramadan fasts for the two years, 2007 and 2008, that he was in the Valley. Combined impact of the above actions subtly influenced local public opinion, and the people now started viewing the rail project as being in their interest. This statesman-like approach played a vital role in the timely commissioning of various phases of Kashmir Valley Railway Project.

Technically too he stamped his brilliance by personally monitoring and handling the most difficult tasks, such as moving heavy and awkward loads on transporter trailers even where it was deemed not feasible by core railway engineers, by drawing upon his experience of moving heavy bridging equipment in difficult terrain. He personally set up a Project Management Information System using PRIMAVERA software tool for effective monitoring of 312 separate contracts under the overall project in his charge.

The project under his charge was significant with overall value of approximately INR 340 Crores and also entailed constructing Budgam Yard, the largest in Ferozepur Division of Northern Railways. Phase 1 of the project was inaugurated in 2008 by the Prime Minister himself, signalling the criticality of the work.

His paper on "Load Testing of Composite Girder Bridge," being used by the railways for the first time in Kashmir Valley, was awarded the gold medal by CMD, IRCON in 2008.

As Joint General Manager, he was given independent charge, reporting directly to Headquarters in Delhi, and given enhanced financial powers.

As the icing on the cake, he was also offered permanent absorption into IRCON and a transfer to their prestigious IRCON-RITES Rail project in Mozambique in Africa.

In the words of Naresh, "As a diehard Olive Green personality, the biggest and most far-reaching impact of deputation with IRCON was my technical learning and confidence. Boundary management, breaking work silos, interpretation of rules and managing internal group dynamics were skill sets, which proved to be of immense help in ensuring success in my second innings."

Changing the Uniform

In 2008, while still with IRCON project, Naresh applied for release from the army which was finally secured in August 2009.

By September 2009, Naresh joined Soma Enterprise Ltd., a Hyderabad-based market leader in PPP-based infrastructure projects, as Head of Planning of their Highways Division, at Gurgaon.

Naresh recollects, "From a mere civil engineering degree from CME, to one of the most challenging railway projects in J&K with a semi-government organisation IRCON, to highways project with a private sector Soma Enterprise Ltd., it was a formidable journey. I could not have asked for a smoother transition from the army to the corporate sector."

Corporate Innings

Naresh had his hands full in planning and monitoring the 291 km Panipat-Jalandhar highway six laning, 93.5 km Kishengarh-Beawar Highway four laning, 132 km Surat-Hazira to Maharashtra border highway four laning, 17.2 km International Container Transshipment Terminus Cochin Port connectivity, 192.4 km Varanasi-Aurangabad Highway construction, and 168 km Hyderabad-Bangalore four laning project.

Soma Enterprise was using Microsoft Project software tool and had engaged a USA-based company for providing planning support. Here again Naresh used his innovation skills to develop one of the most detailed project plans in MS Project software, for the Kishengarh-Beawar Highway project, encompassing more than 10,000 activities. It was a feat appreciated even by Microsoft team in India. Familiarisation with varied project management software was a skill which would be of immense help to Naresh in his later entrepreneurial journey.

"My three major achievements with Soma enterprise were my skills in handling highway projects planning as a whole, planning of the Kishengarh-Beawar Highway four laning project and my study program with Harvard Business School. The latter gave me confidence to start my own project consultancy business," says Naresh.

In March 2011, Naresh proceeded to register BBV Consultant LLP with a friend as partner and quit Soma Enterprise. Naresh offers two reasons for taking the entrepreneur route. "I wanted to harness my intellectual capability in a broader way, and as a consultant I would have full freedom of work with no outer boundaries. Also, I had confidence in my ability to connect with people and was in professional touch with contacts in foreign countries from my IRCON and Soma Enterprise days," says Naresh.

With the incorporation of BBV Consultant, Naresh forayed into the field of entrepreneurship as an international consultant in the field of infrastructure development. National Housing Board, Sri Lanka was planning a 44-acre housing project, in PPP mode, in their picturesque hill station Kandy in central Sri Lanka. Beginning from May to December 2011, Naresh spent the next six months in attempting to secure the approval of the Government of Sri Lanka for undertaking the project. But bureaucratic obduracy finally won the day, and Naresh stopped pursuing the project. Money was lost, but important contacts had been established in the Sri Lanka Government, which would subsequently leverage him to the post of Executive Vice Chairman, Indo-Sri Lanka Chamber of Commerce & Industry.

Naresh's partner in business lacked staying power to sustain losses and quit BBV Consultant in 2012. Naresh's spouse, Sandhya, stepped in as the new partner. The financial situation became even more strained, but he continued, duly supported by Sandhya.

In 2012, in a bid to shore up the finances, Naresh explored railways advisory services and investment opportunities in Oman and Saudi Arabia, but to no avail. Naresh also began undertaking guest lecture assignments. Faculty of Management Studies at University of Delhi, Indian Management Institute and Fore School of Business are some of the business schools where he taught. His subject "Project Management and Project Management Software" was unique and in great demand. These guest lectures and a study assignment by a USA-based company on cold chain logistics in India kept the revenue flowing just to sustain the operations.

In 2013, Naresh got his first major breakthrough when BBV Consultant was engaged by two major Indian companies as an Energy Project Advisor to bid for a 1000 MW Thermal Power and 200 MW Solar Project in Myanmar, with an estimated project cost of INR 6000 Crores. The bid process dragged on for almost two years before it finally fell through in April 2015. By 2016, the company was earning enough to enable it to continue working from Connaught Place.

An India-based diamond cutting and polishing company entered into an advisory agreement with Naresh, in mid-2015, to act on their behalf for advising them on partnering with governments in Africa in mining and processing before rough diamonds are brought to India for cutting and polishing. Naresh wistfully says, "This has been the only time when I have had the opportunity of sitting with kgs and kgs of diamonds all around me."

As a consultant in the international space, Naresh was always on the lookout for new opportunities. Innovo Network Ltd., Thatcham, United Kingdom had been established in the Business Development and Services domain and served multiple business sectors. It was a startup with a unique business model. It harnessed capacities of professionals on time contract with deferred payment based on the new value created by the work. In September 2014, Naresh joined it as PPP infrastructure development expert and provided support online. The advantages of networking in the international arena was not lost on Naresh, and he made determined efforts to widen and institutionalise his network.

During professional interactions with the Indian and Sri Lankan High Commissioners, the absence of a trade body to foster trade relations between the two countries was felt. Dr Krishan Kumar, ex IAS and ex Minister in the Government of India, Lt Gen Rakesh Loomba, veteran of Indian Army and Naresh came together to fill this void. With due approvals from the two governments, they incorporated "Indo-Sri Lanka Chamber of Commerce and Industry" as a Section 8 company in March 2016. The bespoke Chamber of commerce was inaugurated in May 2016 by the Minister of State General VK Singh. The High Commissioners of the two countries were also present. The chamber was also launched in Colombo, Sri Lanka in October 2016. The chamber is highly active and has already pushed projects in Energy, Pharmaceutical and Agriculture sectors.

UNECE, with headquarters in Palais des Nations, Geneva, Switzerland is actively pursuing e-sustainable development goals.

In 2015, they were looking for pro-bono experts to assist them in formulating, drafting and releasing PPP standards for Railways. The services were required to be pro bono. Naresh was quick to offer his services and was taken on board as one of the twenty-odd members in the Railway PPP Standard Project Team. Subsequently, he was asked to assume the leadership of the team at the stage when the member nations had sent their comments on the draft, and those were to be integrated in the document being drafted. Naresh worked hard, and his efforts bore fruit with the release of "Standard on Public Private Partnerships in Railways," in November 2018. It is a twenty-two-page advisory with due review and consent of member nations. UNECE specially acknowledged the contribution of Naresh. He was also invited to make a presentation to the team drafting legal framework for "Railway Movement between Europe and Asia." Brand quality of BBV Consulting had got an international fillip.

While working on the railways project with UNECE, the PPP experts got to discuss the lack of an International Association of PPP professionals. There was general consensus to get the PPP professionals from diverse fields as Finance, Legal, Civil Engineers, Public Policy and Informal Sector on one platform and also further UN sustainable development agenda. This led to the formation of The World Association of PPP Units and Professionals, with registered office at 22 Rue de Rothschild, Geneva 1202, Switzerland. It was formally launched in November 2018 in the presence of representatives from ninety-three countries. The active contribution of Naresh in setting up and mobilising the professionals was duly recognised when he was elected to be Treasurer and Chairman of the Editorial Board of the publications of the association. In the short time frame of under two years, the association has already become an elite networking club with access to most of the governments and a highly influential body in advising, capacity building, hosting regular webinars and other events.

In April 2015, Kathmandu in Nepal was hit by a major earthquake. Naresh was informally approached for expression of interest to engage in a reconstruction project. To execute the assigned task, he set up

Astainable Construction Pvt. Ltd., in 2016, specialising in post-disaster reconstruction. They successfully constructed 100 earthquake-proof permanent shelters in 2018 and continue to work in the niche segment of post-disaster reconstruction worldwide.

Naresh set up Gajanan Innovations Pvt. Ltd., incorporated in November 2018, for providing app-based veterinary connect to cattle owners. The pilot project is running in West Uttar Pradesh. Naresh has engaged with the Uttar Pradesh Government for a formal association to enhance connectivity between government veterinary doctors and cattle owners while at the same time interacting with prospective investors to scale up this business.

The next project which Naresh has taken on is banding the Bana clan onto one common platform. The Bana *parivar* is in the process of organising itself under the umbrella of Bana Foundation, the new age way of doing social work. The first small step is to provide scholarships to deserving meritorious students from the clan. They have already held three annual meetings of the Bana clan, the last one being hosted by Naresh's village in February 2020.

NARESH SPEAKS

Learnings from the armed forces

The basic building block of my learning from the armed forces is sincerity of purpose. From sincerity flows hard work, which in turn necessitates

physical fitness and mental robustness. In the business world the requirement of mental robustness is more important.

Mutual trust and faith are critical for success in any armed forces team; your very life and success of team tasks depends on it. People should be able to trust you. This is the best guarantee for long-term success.

Army has taught me to work with equal ease from the footpath as well as from a seven-star environment.

Difficulties
My biggest difficulty lay in coming to terms with the differences in work culture between the armed forces and the business world, especially in the initial stages. They are so different.

In the armed forces any communication received must be replied to. In the world of business, response to communication is a rare occurrence. Quite often there is no response, unless there is some gain to the affected party. A great deal of time and energy has to be spent to solicit a response.

Agreements/MOUs/Understandings whether written or verbal are just as good as the paper they are written on. More often, the lawyer and arbitration fees are enormous enough to act as a deterrent for veteran entrepreneurs to pursue this course.

I have followed a simple business fundamental of not booking a profit until and unless the bankers confirm the credit.

In the business world, trust does not always beget trust. So, you have to be judicious in safeguarding your interest.

For payments and business development trust no one, not even your erstwhile comrades in arms.

Three Major Achievements
Gaining business confidence is one of my biggest achievements. As a PPP Consultant, in multiple spectrums of Infrastructure Development, it has enabled me to develop confidence in my professional abilities.

My association and interactions with UNECE at Geneva, Indo-Sri Lanka Chambers of Commerce and Industry and World Association of PPP Individuals and Units has truly enabled me to develop a deep understanding and value of international business connect.

I have learnt from super intelligent, reputed international business leaders, professional diplomats, bureaucrats, engineers, lawyers and chartered accountants the value of commitment while doing business. This has immensely enriched me to take on any challenge in life.

Advice for the Mad Vets
Understand the difference in professional culture between armed forces and the corporate world.

Outside the armed forces, taking no decision is also a good decision. Bureaucracy has developed it into an art. Hence, earmarking time for follow-through action is important. It is tedious but necessary.

You are good at what you have done in the armed forces. Capitalise on those skills for your business venture. Your experience will add more value to your business venture rather than extra degrees and diplomas.

Incidentally, I do not recommend seeking premature retirement from the armed forces unless you have a well-thought-out, adequately-funded and suitably-procured plan of business.

Options for the Mad Vets to Undertake New Ventures
There is no general rule to a successful business startup. It is dependent on your area of expertise and availability of capital for your venture.

If you have to associate with an existing business, then be a sincere learner.

Philosophy Towards Life
Chase credibility, not money.

An armed forces officer carries credibility in the eyes of the others. Build on it. It's the safest route to financial success in the long term.

Personal Qualities that Have Helped You
Self-discipline and self-motivation are my biggest drivers.

Paying due respect to advice from my spouse, more so, as she is also my business partner.

Future Vision

I am now more inclined to progress in industry leadership roles through my association with UNECE at Geneva, Indo-Sri Lanka Chambers of Commerce and Industry and World Association of PPP Units and Professionals.

During the lockdown, I authored an article on "Post Pandemic Human Resource Paradigm in PPP Projects" and was co-moderator in an international webinar on post-pandemic impact on various PPP sectors held on 29 April 2020. This webinar was co-sponsored by APMG and World Association of PPP Units and Professionals.

Bana Foundation is also an area of active interest for me, and I intend to devote more time and energy in building it up.

The Future of India

I look to the future of India in the near term of under three years, medium term of ten years and long term.

In the near term, management of minorities will be a challenge that has to be accomplished with skill and judiciousness. It will have a major impact on international relations and consequently on business environment. Low hydrocarbon energy import bills, substantial enhancement of self-sufficiency in renewable energies and a youthful and skilled demographic profile should pay heavy dividends.

India is also well poised to be invited to fill Human Resource openings in Europe post adverse impact of Covid-19.

The widespread impact of Covid-19 pandemic is likely to bring urgent focus on the health of our ailing agrarian sector. I foresee removal of archaic laws, introduction of efficient new technologies and creation of greater job opportunities in the agrarian economy, in the near term.

In the medium term, while we may miss the target for a US Dollars 3 trillion economy by 2022, we will be well poised to be a US Dollars 10 trillion economy by 2030.

The long-term prospects of the Indian economy are even brighter, as it is forecasted to be the second largest economy in the world by 2050.

One Mantra for the Mad Vets

I have always retained the trust of my seniors with whom I have worked. If you commit to something, then ensure delivery even at the cost of financial loss. Trust is difficult to regain, whereas financial loss can be offset in the long term.

Willingness to Mentor Mad Vets

I am always open to mentor the veterans coming to me for business advice. In fact, I have already undertaken group presentations for veterans as and when invited.

On Role of Spouse

Sandhya is a very positive and supportive life and business partner for me, and she fully backed my decision to leave the highly lucrative private sector job to start my own business consultancy. Even in 2012, when I seriously considered winding up my business venture, it was Sandhya who expressed faith in my capabilities and motivated me to continue.

Initially, she kept herself fully committed to raising our two daughters, though I did merit a hot cup of tea from her, even in the cold winter mornings when I had to leave early for my golf. The household and the progress of the children continue to be her first love.

Now she supervises the HR support functions and also handles our office procurements.

* * *

Thoughts on keeping the spirit young

THROUGH THE JOURNEY OF TIME, LIFE RENEWS AT FIFTY

Listen to hear my whispers in the Wind,
Look into Time to see my footprints in Sand,
The whispers and footprints merge in Time.

I wonder at the Journey and cherish it again,
And the thought emerges that the Journey is so young,
Beyond the Dunes the Mountains beckon.

Wonder at the scape and new pastures I see,
As pathless wonder stretches beyond,
Realisation dawns it's the Journey that counts.

Horizon is wide, but the Mind goes beyond,
Gravity shackles the Body but never the Mind,
Give flight to the Mind, and the Body goes along.

In unexplored vistas, the paths don't matter,
The Journey's end is the destination you reach,
You have engraved your Journey on the rocks of Time.

- Col RS Sidhu

* * *

New Age Technology Entrepreneur

. . . .

"There is a child within me even today."

- Col Sunil Prem

Topped his college in pre-university exams in 1980 and overall 15th in the 290-plus colleges of Panjab University.

Awarded the silver medal for being 'Best in Academics', with a new academics record, a bronze medal for "Best Overall" performance and "Overall Best Army Cadet" in NDA in 1983.

Awarded the gold medal for being 'First in the Order of Merit' at the IMA, in 1984.

Secured first rank, with distinction, on Young Officers (Engineers) Course at CME in 1985.

Best in 'Special Mission' in Commando Course Officers at Commando School in 1985 and 'Platoon Weapons Course' at Infantry School, Mhow in 1985.

Awarded gold medal, with a new academics record, in B Tech in Electrical Engineering 1987-90 at CME, Pune.

Secured 10 out of 10 Cumulative Point Index (CPI) in M Tech from Indian Institute of Technology, Kanpur in 1994.

Awarded distinction at Army Command & Staff Course at Fort Queenscliff, Australia in 1998.

Stood first, with distinction in Nuclear Biological Chemical Warfare Staff Officers Course at CME in 2002.

Co-founder of Arnima Ventures LLP, incorporated in 2009, in the field of anti-terrorism infrastructure and honoured with Certificate of Appreciation from the Home Minister in 2012.

Co-founder of Navyug Info Solutions Pvt. Ltd., incorporated in June 2010, in the field of custom software development, with annual revenue of INR seven crores and winner of Army Make in India Challenge, DISC III Chapter of Innovations for Defence Exhibition (IDEX), 2020.

Founder of Brisk Olive Business Solutions Pvt. Ltd., incorporated in September 2019, in the field of Recruitment Services, largescale on-ground Surveys, Audits, Projects, Promotions and Training, with over one crore current revenue and targeted revenue of more than seven crores for FY 2020-21.

Co-founder of Global Harmony Trust, an NGO, registered in 2010, in the field of corporate social responsibility, with a mission to make the world a better place to live in by promoting solar sustainability, green environment and disaster mitigation.

This is Colonel Sunil Prem for you. You can be forgiven to presume that Sunil Prem with the above accomplishments and Sunil Prem a child who was happy securing 28th position out of twenty-eight students successively, in early primary classes, are two different personalities with the same name!

Early Life

Sunil Prem, born in January 1964 in Delhi, was the younger of two siblings. His father was a sales professional and mother a teacher in a government school in Delhi, who left her job to raise her two children. The family had roots in Lyallpur in West Punjab, now in Pakistan, and on partition of the country, moved to Delhi as refugees. Their father's company would move him frequently from one town to another, and the family would move too. As a result, Sunil and his elder brother spent their early years studying in schools at New Delhi, Kathgodam and Faizabad in undivided Uttar Pradesh, Chandigarh, Karnal in Haryana, Meerut in Uttar Pradesh and again Chandigarh.

Sunil, the younger of the two siblings, was a happy-go-lucky child at school. While his elder brother was securing first position in his class, Sunil was comfortable coming last. Whenever their family shifted to a new city, the elder brother passed the entrance exams of the new school and Sunil, true to his self, failed. This posed a decision dilemma for their parents – *how to ensure that both siblings study in the same school?* For the children to study in two different schools involved managing the logistics nightmare of different pick and drop timings, different transport, different holidays and vacation periods. It took a herculean effort by the parents to achieve the feat of getting their two children enrolled in the same school despite disparate academic performance. So, when Sunil again secured the 28th rank out of twenty-eight students in a semester of Class III, his father decided to take action. He began to tutor him. It was at this opportune moment for Sunil that his uncle, an army man, came visiting. The latter directed Sunil to write "I will come first in my class" in his school notebook. With the innocence of an upright child, Sunil requested his uncle to let him substitute the word "First" with "Third." The proposed amendment by Sunil Prem was overruled by his uncle. Later, Sunil's elder brother, all of 11 years old, also chipped in with a sibling-to-sibling advice of "stop listening to parents and concentrate on enjoying life." This, Sunil says, has been the best advice he has ever received in his life.

To everyone's surprise, he secured third position in the next exam in Class III. It was a transformational moment in the life of Sunil Prem. He realised his own capability to achieve whatever he set his mind to do. He also realised that one usually does well at what one truly enjoys. He never looked back thereafter.

While still in primary school, Sunil developed a fondness for reading fiction with interest in the action genre. Over a period of time, this kindled an interest in joining the armed forces. In time, he appeared for the entrance examination for NDA, Pune.

Life in the Army

After qualifying in the entrance examination for NDA, he joined the institution as a cadet in June 1980. Swimming holds a very high value while assessing the leadership potential of trainees. Cadets unable to achieve laid-down performance standards invite relegation and even withdrawal for repeated defaults. Sunil, at the time of joining, was a non-swimmer and could just splash around to save his life. During the second term, Sunil and his squad were taken to the swimming pool for introductory 10-metre board jump. Sunil was one of a small group of volunteers for jumping from the 10-metre board. Sunil's jump was, however, at an awkward angle. In the words of Sunil, "When my turn came, I too stepped out onto the board and jumped without a thought. And I fell flat! The water hit me so hard in my groin that it felt as if I was dying! Our instructor pushed a pole towards me. And I clung to that and came out of the pool."

Approximately a month later, Sunil and his batch were due for their assessment in the 7-metre board jump. Sunil was quite confident when he climbed up to the board. When Sunil's turn came, he just froze on the board. Sunil says, "I was scared to death! There were a few other cadets too who had not jumped. We were all moved down progressively to 5 metres and then to 3 metres. At every stage, I found myself unable to jump. Finally, I was standing on the 1 meter board and there too I could not jump! I don't know how long I stood there. I was dimly aware of the instructor yelling and shouting at me for being a coward. Then, with a snap, I came out of my stupor and my brain began to function. I suddenly became conscious of the fact that even a child can't get hurt jumping from a 1-metre board. Therefore, my fear had to be unreal! Besides, it was better to die than be seen as a coward. That very moment, I just sprinted off the 1-metre board, straight on to the 10 meter one and jumped! I have always been thankful for not having jumped from that 1-metre board. For nothing could have showed to me the *irrationality* of fear more clearly than that. I realised that fear is the result of anticipating the worst which one can imagine, but not being ready for it."

In June 1983, Sunil successfully completed his training at NDA. He was awarded the silver medal for being "Best in Academics" with a new academics record, a bronze medal for "Best Overall" performance and "Overall Best Army Cadet."

After graduating from NDA, Sunil Prem joined IMA, Dehradun. Here he was awarded the gold medal for being 'First in the Overall Order of Merit.' Sunil, due to his interest in technology, opted for Corps of Engineers, more popularly known as Sappers. In June 1984, Sunil completed his training at IMA. He was happy to be allotted his choice of arm and was dispatched to Bengal Engineering Group (BEG) at Roorkee. After a month, he moved to attend YO's Course at CME, Pune. Here again he stood first on the course with Delta grading. In January 1985, he was posted to 237 Engineer Regiment, which would be his parent unit. The regiment was then located at Ferozepur and Sunil spent most of his time as a subaltern happily with his troops on training, operational deployments and doing mandatory courses.

The Corps of Engineers are tasked to provide battlefield mobility to own troops as well as laying obstacles to restrict mobility of the enemy. One of the most dangerous tasks assigned to them is to lay and retrieve minefields. To maintain surprise, the minefields are almost always laid in the hours of darkness. The alignment of the minefield is first plotted on the map. The map coordinates are then marked on the ground. Several parties are required to work in closest cooperation to dig holes exactly as per marking, assemble, carry, place and then arm the mines. Thereafter, they camouflage the minefield. The whole procedure is most carefully recorded because of the underlying principle of "layer of the mine retrieves the mine." The highest level of map reading standards and navigation is the key. But the most important quality for a Sapper to lay mines is to have ice in his veins. Even the slightest of misalignment or drop in concentration can lead to fatalities or much worse, maiming for life.

Sunil, along with his team, was tasked to lay live mines during operational training. They laid mines over three consecutive nights without a break, as day time was spent in preparing mines for the next night's task. On the fourth morning, they were tasked to retrieve these mines, a task which is usually done during daytime. After the first strip of mines had been lifted, tallying of mines laid and retrieved showed an error of one mine less. In his urgency to ensure that no one stepped on the live mine, and through sheer oversight, Sunil Prem walked into the live minefield! It was some metres before he realised his error. His team stood still with all eyes on him. Says Sunil, "My Sappers were watching me intently. As their leader, I could not show fear in front of my men. Reputations carry in the army for a lifetime! So, whether foolish or stupid, I decided to walk on. I knew that I could be maimed or killed. It was the first time in my life I sensed a physical icy chill in my heart as I walked on trying to look nonchalant. And I was thankful for the earlier opportunity provided to me to conquer my fear at the NDA swimming pool."

After spending a year at Ferozepur, 237 ENGINEERS was moved to the North East in Arunachal Pradesh. Here he came face to face with his first experience of solitude. Sunil recalls, "I was deployed on a post near a little village called Menchukha in Arunachal Pradesh, nestled in the Himalayan ranges. I was there with my company, building bunkers, tracks and bridges for our forces deployed along the Chinese border. It rained or snowed a lot in Menchukha, the temperatures touched minus twenty degrees centigrade, and the wind was a killer. It would blow off corrugated iron roofing sheets like leaves! For days at a stretch we could only sit, waiting for the weather to improve and for work to re-start. TV, radio and such other gadgets did not work."

"Silence of the wild was my constant companion. Slowly I started enjoying the 'sound' of silence. I also learnt to introspect and find answers from within."

After a year's stay at Menchukha, Sunil moved to CME, Pune for his B Tech in Civil Engineering. This was also the time when Sunil was married to Archana, which brought greater stability in his personal life. As had now become the norm for him, Sunil topped the degree course.

In 1992, Sunil was assigned to Indian Institute of Technology, Kanpur for M Tech where he secured a 10/10 Cumulative Point Index (CPI). Sunil recalls, "Surprisingly, IIT was loads of fun and educational at the same time. I realised there that our Army education and training, which we felt was not applicable outside, was actually quite transferable and relevant. Besides, perhaps the professors were a bit lenient with us married, uniformed fellows attending the course."

His next memorable posting was as an instructor at the National Defence Academy. Sunil recalls it as one of his most valuable tenures as he got on ground with young cadets aspiring to be officers in the Indian Army. He loved getting on the ground with the cadets. "I realised," he says, "that I had a tremendous and humbling responsibility, for I would be in a position to influence young and highly impressionable minds. And I tried to build myself into the best version of myself that I could. I do not know whether my cadets realised it, but I was getting trained along with them!"

While at NDA, he was selected to attend the Army Command and Staff Course, Fort Queenscliff, Australia. The year was 1998, and India carried out testing of its nuclear weapons at Pokharan in Rajasthan. The operation was codenamed 'Smiling Buddha.' It created an international furore resulting in economic sanctions. Australia broke off relations with India, and Sunil had to return. He was then detailed to attend the Defence Services Staff College Course at Wellington, in India.

In February 2001, Sunil was posted for one year with the United Nations Mission in Kinshasa, Democratic Republic of Congo. He was appointed as the team leader of a United Nations team of four international officers. For the first six months, he was stationed in Pweto, a little Congolese village just North of Zambia. Their mission was to oversee a United Nations mandated demilitarisation between the RPA rebel and government forces. Pweto was a mere dot on the demilitarisation line that stretched hundreds of miles to the Northwest, up to Congo's border with the Central African Republic to the North.

The demilitarisation zone was often violated by both sides, and sporadic acts of violence were common. The value of life in a war-ravaged country is cheap and senseless killing is common. Apart from trying to prevent or report such incidents, there was very little to do. Most of the time was spent in solitude and deep thought.

"Like in Menchukha, there was no TV and the radio did not work. We could not drive more than a few kilometres on either side of the camp. There were no roads, just dirt tracks. Crocodile-infested rivers lay across these tracks and could be crossed only on boats. Every fortnight, a UN replenishment flight would land at a rough airstrip close to us. It would quickly unload supplies, while the pilot smoked and moved off to the next post. The daily high-points were the short reconnaissance patrols and the radio-set being switched on each evening. Within our team of four members, one was usually away on leave or sick with malaria. Besides, the members were all from different countries. Most spoke French. For those six months, each one of us was practically alone. I walked, exercised, read, wrote and thought. And I thought a lot during those days," says Sunil.

Sunil is philosophical while musing, "The time spent at Menchukha and Pweto taught me the value of meditative silence. This is the kind of silence which means putting away all thoughts of the past and all worries about the future. The body, mind and emotions fall silent, and one begins to live in the present. I learnt the true meaning of meditation, and many things fell into perspective during these periods. I realised the importance of leading my life the way I saw it and not being stopped from attempting to accomplish what I myself wanted to do."

From Pweto, Sunil moved to a UN local headquarters in Kalemie towards the North. Again, there was not much to do, and to keep himself occupied, he would volunteer for most out-of-camp reconnaissance missions. On one such mission, he was tasked to investigate the alleged burning of an entire village named Manono by government troops. This village was close to Lake Tanganyika in rebel-held territory. Sunil and his team were assigned a helicopter to proceed to the site. He was accompanied by a small unarmed reconnaissance team and a local guide.

Sunil recalls it vividly, "Every village looked the same from high up in the air. The usual method of identifying a village was for our Russian pilots to circle over it till the local guide would yell 'No, this is not the one!' We would then move on to the next likely village, and the routine would be repeated. We finally identified Manono from the smoke rising from some huts that were still smouldering. The area outside the village was bush land, with limited ground visibility. When we were just 20 metres off the ground, over 50 heavily armed rebels rushed out of the bushes, screaming and aiming their weapons at us. A majority were just boys or little more than boys. We were so close that I could make out their fingers tensing on the triggers. I had no time to think. The pilots had stopped the descent. That, I felt, could be fatal. If even one of the rebels pressed the trigger, all others would open up. So I yelled at the pilots to continue a steady descent. Then I leaned out of the helicopter, trying to act and look as confident as I could. As the helicopter touched the ground, I just grabbed a few papers and began to yell at the rebel soldiers, waving those papers in their faces. I was certain that none of the rebels could hear me over the noise of the rotor blades. That was not my aim, because I was yelling stuff and nonsense! Besides, I was yelling in English, while the RPA spoke French! But I continued my yelling and acting outraged, waving those papers all the while. That show of aggression worked. When one acts confident, others assume that you have a reason to be confident. I could see the rebels trigger fingers loosening. Then someone pushed ahead from among the rebels. It was the local rebel leader. Death missed us by the proverbial whisker."

The incident had a deep impact on the life of Sunil. He says, "It taught me an important thing about life. We hear this lesson all the time, but it truly sinks in when one is faced with such a situation. Our life is beautiful and yet so fragile. It hangs by a slender thread which can snap at any moment. We as individuals usually have no control over that. It could happen right now, at this moment, due to any reason. So why worry about any tomorrow, which might never come? So within the limits of being sensible, each day must be lived now, and it must be lived to realise one's own potential, whatever that be. That is all there is to life!"

A year after his return, Sunil was assigned to attend Nuclear Biological Chemical Warfare Course at CME. He again topped the course with a Delta grading. Eighteen years later, when asked to share his perspective on India's preparedness to withstand a biological attack, in the backdrop of the Covid-19 pandemic, Sunil responds, "A biological weapon attack and the current Covid-19 virus both share a common characteristic – both are extremely difficult to control. This is why biological weapons are so rarely used. This pandemic has brought the world to its knees. As Robert Burns puts it, 'The best laid schemes of mice and men have come to naught within months!' This is not unexpected in a globalised world, where everything affects everything else. Being flexible and adaptive to situations is the solution, rather than trying to apply old templates mindlessly to new problems. On this very assumption, one of my companies had created the Soldier2ndlife network. Soldiers are used to managing crises of all kinds, and they are the best operations people that you can think of. Such a network is very relevant in today's world. Like during the Covid-19 crisis too, we offered our services to the government, conducted trainings, distributed food and even manufactured masks, which we distributed through our soldiers' wives network!"

For the next few years after returning from Africa, Sunil served on the staff of a formation, followed by being Second in Command, and then as the Commanding Officer of 237 Engineer Regiment, the unit he was commissioned into. One of the major operational commitments of 237 Engineer Regiment during his command tenure was to remove the leftover mines laid during Operation Parakram. Under his able command, this most difficult assignment was accomplished without suffering any casualty. Another equally challenging task was constructing a track in thickly wooded and hilly, insurgency-prone area North of Poonch. The tasks were very challenging, and the regiment performed exceptionally well.

After completing command of his unit, Sunil was posted as the Colonel General Staff of a Division, which was equipped and tasked for offensive role. It was a time of great learning for him. But he also missed being with his officers and troops, and could see that this phase of his professional life was now past. He decided to quit.

Sunil reasons out his decision to leave the army, "I soon became restless in the staff posting. My children were now studying in higher grades where continuity of school mattered. I did not look forward to the prospect of staying away from my family for the next six years. All those who mattered to me opposed my decision to leave the army at a time when they felt I was doing 'well.' I followed my own heart and moved out to try my hand at the challenge of entrepreneurship."

Change of Uniform

In April 2007, Sunil moved to Delhi along with his family and joined a six-month business certificate course with Management Development Institute, Gurgaon. And on completion of his certification course, in September 2007, Sunil bade adieu to the army after 27-and-a-half years. He, however, only shed the exterior Olive Green covers; his inner core would always remain Olive Green. He was now ready to match his theoretical brilliance with practical application in the entrepreneur sector.

Simultaneously, Sunil received a break when he was approached by a friend for starting a partnership venture in the software technology sector. There were to be equal partners – three persons eventually. Says Sunil, "This seemed like a Godsend opportunity to me. I had developed a passion for technology. It was the future. I was raring to get back into action, and there was also this confidence and certainty that I would succeed somehow. Even if I did fail, at least I would have tried."

By now, the software company, Wien Tech Systems Pvt. Ltd., was already registered and Sunil became a "partner" in it. He knew nothing of the outside world, so being partner to him meant that he was actually helping the company and also putting in his money. He asked for no commitments on paper and instead reposed implicit faith in the first partner. This naïve attitude was to prove costly but would also be an invaluable learning to him later on.

Since the software venture needed money to grow, Sunil simultaneously joined a Real Estate Development organisation as General Manager, Human Resource & Administration for a year, and continued to support the software company from outside. He followed it up with another tenure of one year as Vice President Planning & Training with WLCI at New Delhi, which worked in the field of Post Graduate Education in Business, Fashion, Design and Media.

Entrepreneur Projects

In the words of Sunil, about his first company, "I spent on the company liberally from my savings, giving whenever required, not asking for any proofs and not keeping much account. Then one fine day my partner said that he wanted to move out with the product, on which we had spent all our money and effort, and create his own company. To my question about all the money that I had spent, he answered, 'What money?'"

The issue was taking an ugly turn. Then fate intervened. Within a few days of this, Sunil met with a late-night accident while driving back home. Sunil recalls, "It was just short of midnight, and I was worked up, thinking about all that was going on while driving back from office. The roads were deserted, and I was going through a 4-way crossing, lost in my thoughts and emotions. Suddenly there was a huge crash, as a goods trailer, coming from the ninety-degree direction, rammed into the rear of my car. The impact was so hard that the car just flew. Fortunately, that impact at the rear sent the car into a spin, which probably absorbed a major part of the momentum. To cut it short, while my car was wrecked, I came out of this incident, shaken but largely uninjured. My second partner, who was following behind in his own car, came to my assistance. We left the wrecked car at the site and began to walk shakily by the side of the road. It was right there walking by the side of the road that the two of us decided to let go of the past, those three years of effort and money spent on that company, to start afresh. It was the wisest decision we took. Instead of fighting a senseless, ugly battle with our third partner, we decided to just let go of the past and move on. I now call all the money that I spent on that company as the fees for my 'street MBA', and I am only half-joking!"

In June 2010, Sunil along with Sanjeev Kumar, his second partner, incorporated Navyug Infosolutions Pvt. Ltd. at NCR Delhi. Later, a third person, Jyotsna Ahuja, joined them at the Board of Directors as an equal partner. The chosen field of operations for the company was customised software development.

Says Sunil, "For the first four months there were no orders. We literally danced when we got our first order of INR 5 lakhs. We did not draw any salary for the first sixteen months. Money went out from home, instead of coming in. Then I began drawing INR 30,000 salary per month for almost two years, and then INR 70,000 for a while more, before getting to the stage where we directors of the company could draw decent salaries."

Sunil continues, "This time, when we started Navyug, we had no money at all. In fact, we were heavily in debt! But help poured in from all sides. A number of friends invested in us. A number of employees from the old company decided to work with us. After that first order, our company started rolling. After that, there was no looking back. This incident taught me the value of goodwill. One can lose money. But if one has created goodwill in life, one never lacks help, money or anything!"

Navyug's products and solutions are based on the Internet of Things, Artificial Intelligence, Web and Mobile Applications. Their in-house design and development facility includes state-of-the-art equipment, including 3D printers. They already have an impressive client list spread over USA, Europe, West Asia, Singapore and of course India. The most significant indicator of their superb product quality and services is that

70% of their clients are long term, with continuing work through long-term business tie-ups.

The crowning achievement of Navyug Info Solutions, to date, is their success at Innovations for Defence Exhibition (IDEX), 2020. This is one of the most prestigious events organised under the government's 'Make in India' plan. The user requirement for the proposed product is shared by the Indian Defence Forces, in advance, with the interested competitors. Each competitor is required to demonstrate the feasibility plan for the design and development of the proposed product. The competitors are then graded on the basis of design and feasibility. The winners are then provided with a grant of INR 1.5 Crore, with matching funding by the competitor to develop the solution within the next 12 to 18 months or so. For the 2020 IDEX Army Challenge, there were forty-plus competitors in the field, and Navyug Info Solutions was selected as one of the five winners of the Army Make in India Challenge, DISC III Chapter of IDEX 2020. The product to be developed is Identify Friend Foe system for combat vehicles – tanks, infantry combat vehicles, etc. – of Indian Army's Mechanised Forces.

Sunil is the CEO of the company, Sanjeev Kumar handles Research & Development, and Jyotsna Ahuja is responsible for Project Delivery. The annual revenues have already touched INR 7 Crores. Talking about the future plans of the organisation, Sunil says, "In the short term, we look forward to further expand the capabilities of our team of 80-plus members, for customised software development services. Our long-term focus is on product development. That is where our hearts lie."

Besides Navyug, Sunil began surveying the market for available opportunities in tune with his skill sets. His experience as an army engineer led him to focus on the scourge of terrorism and IEDs, the favourite weapon of the terrorists. Every year, the security forces suffer casualties from IED-related incidents. There was need for creating modern training infrastructure where the security forces could train in counter-IED operations. Again, Sunil was fortunate. His past goodwill in the armed forces led another Sapper officer Col Navneet Mittal to offer him an equal partnership along with a third army friend and colleague. Sunil says about Col Navneet Mittal, "He is senior to me, and I respect his professional competence a lot. But most importantly, he is one of the largest hearted persons I have ever met!"

So Arnima Ventures LLP was incorporated in Pune, with three partners, towards the end of 2009. It is the privileged recipient of a Certificate of Appreciation from the Home Minister, in 2012, for developing Central Reserve Police Force (CRPF) Institution of IED Management, at Talegaon in Pune. It was the first such facility outside of the armed forces. Arnima Ventures has built counter-IED training facilities for practically every large security organisation in India – the Indian Army, Navy, CRPF, Special Forces, Intelligence organisations, police forces, even airports and airlines. Their solutions include state-of-the-art software and Internet of Things solutions, Tactical Engagement Training Simulators, Remotely Operated Vehicles, IED Model Rooms, Laboratories and Field Kits. The company is also diversified into system integration and execution of turn-key LED and solar projects, and they have facilities at Noida, Uttar Pradesh and Pune, Maharashtra.

Apart from Col Navneet Mittal and Sunil, currently, Arnima has two more partners – Lt Col Sandeep Misra from Armoured Corps and Maj Jaideep Singh Chandi from Infantry. Navneet as Chairman handles Strategy, Sunil is the CEO, Sandeep is the COO, and Jaideep is on the Board of Directors.

Sunil exudes confidence while saying, "Anti-Terrorism and Counter-IED Training is a very small but niche segment, and Arnima Ventures LLP is its exclusive leader. We started with equity from friends and family, and within a decade our annual revenue has already crossed more than INR four crores. We have paid up all our debts, and we do not owe anyone a penny."

One of the big dreams of Sunil is to help bring in transformation in India through the power of the Defence Veterans community. He had been working on this idea for over 5 years in parallel, and to realise his dream, Sunil incorporated Brisk Olive Business Solutions Pvt. Ltd. at Noida in September 2019. It has two verticals. One is to provide recruitment services for hiring of veterans. The second is to provide nationwide, very largescale, feet-on-ground services in the fields of project management, turn-key projects, process audits, surveys, investigations, training and social impact schemes.

Sunil is the CEO, and this time his business partner is also his life partner, Archana. Sunil has set an ambitious target of orders to the value of INR 7 crores for 2020-21.

Its 'Soldier2ndLife' initiative is already India's largest network of ex-defence personnel and spouses – with over 100,000 persons on ground and 20,000 plus online. The company is providing jobs and services to armed forces veterans. It also has the largest number of on-demand, feet-on-ground, service providers in the country.

On the 'Soldier2ndLife' initiative, Sunil says, "Well it is a personal challenge, as well as passion, to create immense value for the country and for our society through the latent and unutilised talents of our Veterans and their spouses."

While peering into his entrepreneurial future, Sunil says, "In Brisk Olive, the vision is to help transform India through the power of the ex-soldiers' community. While at Navyug and Arnima Ventures, we shall continue doing what we do – providing reliable, quality services to clients around the world – on time, every time! But our focus shall now be in the field of Technology. We have a long way to go as yet. We have experimented with a lot of things. We have made products, failed at some and made some progress in others. And we have learnt. I see ourselves making more products and solutions in future. Our focus, as always, is to provide massive value in things that improve society."

When asked to peer into his entrepreneur journey with hindsight, Sunil reminisces, "I liked software. But the advice of my well-wishers was not to start a software company, because I did not know software. I chose to do so because I wanted to. Even if I failed at least I would have tried. Today, I can talk on technology to my children and to people across generations. So maybe in my old age, I will not be left wondering about where the world is going."

He further adds, "Initially, there was little planning. However, in the past few years, I have spent heavily, in terms of money and time, learning about every aspect of business – sales, marketing, digital marketing, operations, support operations, etc. When one has to run a business, it is best to learn everything about it. In a similar vein, it took me six years to create the network of soldiers. I thought that the values with which soldiers retired were going underutilised by the world outside. So I kept at it, despite all downs. Again it would not have mattered even if I had not succeeded. It would have mattered to me if I had never tried."

On being asked about finding gainful time for three different ventures and what he intends to focus on in the future, Sunil smiles and says, "We have put in place strong processes in our ventures, and of course, I keep myself aloof from day-to-day operations. My focus is now on a passion, which I have indulged for over thirty years. It all started with my 'time of solitude' during postings with the UN Mission in DRC of Congo and in Menchukha, Arunachal Pradesh. I became interested in human psychology, and as my interest in the subject grew, I started self-schooling myself in this discipline. For the past twelve years, I have been carrying out focused research. It delves into the patterns that make up an individual and helps them in accomplishing their desired goals, and it deals with bringing awareness about the power of these little patterns to the surface. I am now writing my findings in a book titled *The Power of Conscious Human Patterns*. In brief, it bridges the 'knowing – doing' gap. A renowned publishing house has already signed a contract with me, and I hope that the book is published within a year. From this shall flow my next tentative venture which will be about helping people use the technique of patterns in everyday life. There is a gap between the aspirations and capabilities of individuals and organisations, leading to tensions in the workplace and in life. The resultant tensions can be resolved by either lowering aspirations, which would be unfortunate, or raising capabilities. Training people in identifying and bridging this critical gap shall be the endeavour of my future venture. Because for people to realise their inherent capabilities, which are truly massive, is far easier than they think. I am currently working on the instruments and technique to support this outcome. Let's see how it shapes up."

SUNIL PREM SPEAKS

Learnings from the Army

Life is short, and it is one. So take each day as it comes, and enjoy it.

Focus on issues, and forget about the non-issues (unimportant things). Do what you love and be passionate about it.

Fear is usually an exaggerated imagination, of unknown and known devils, so get over it and get going with what has to be done. Do not laugh at others' fears, for I have felt them too.

Be ever willing to take *"pangas"* (untested ideas). Never be afraid to fail. To have never failed is tantamount to not having explored the boundaries of capabilities.

Have broad enough shoulders to accept responsibility for own actions.

Care for people.

Create massive value. Because value is all that lasts.

Philosophy Towards Life

Doing what you love is the cornerstone to true abundance in life.

Life becomes an adventure when I enjoy it even when the adventure is on, and not just in the subsequent narration of it.

Personal Qualities that Have Helped

Confidence, being myself and having equal respect for self and others.

Passion, so that work never feels like work.

Optimism and not being afraid of trying.

Difficulties and Overcoming Them

Nothing is ever difficult or easy. It is our thoughts that make them so. Our thinking on any issue shapes our attitude towards it, our understanding or lack of it, and choice of the way forward to doing it right.

If we love something, we never find it difficult. If we don't like something or don't know how to do it or don't do it correctly, of course, we will find it *difficult!*

When I started my software company with my friend, I knew very little of software. But I liked it. I also knew that if 20-year-old kids could do it, surely it could not be rocket science. So I dug up the B Tech Computer Science syllabus and started going through it, subject by subject. And I asked anyone who could teach me, even if they might have thought me a fool for asking. So I learnt. Today, I myself maintain the software for my new company, Brisk Olive. And I am writing a program to go along with my book, *The Power of Conscious Human Patterns.*

Impact on Lives of Others

It is my belief that creating massive value for others is the only way of doing things. That value has a way of multiplying and finding its way back to you. But to do things regardless of that return is the paradox that makes absolute sense. That is the essence of the Bhagvad Gita.

Today, my endeavour is to create massive value through varied services that we provide through our companies and through what I do personally.

Work for the soldiers' network, to aggregate their values and connect those values to society.

Advise retiring soldiers on how to make their second lives as great as their first ones.

Advise some entrepreneurs in their entrepreneurial ventures.

Talk about and teach anyone who is interested, about consciously patterning one's life for self-realisation, self-mastery, success and fulfilment.

Major Achievements

Development of the Institute of IED Management at Talegaon, Pune for CRPF by Arnima Ventures LLP is one of our most successful accomplishments. The infrastructure was designed and constructed by us from scratch. On completion of the assignment, in 2012, we were awarded by the Home Minister. This is probably the first and only institute of its kind with the Para Military Forces. Today police forces of over 40 countries are trained here on counter-IED measures and techniques.

Navyug Infosolutions Pvt. Ltd. has designed and prototyped an innovative 'Identification Friend or Foe' system for the Mechanized Forces of the Indian Army. The solution was adjudged the best in the Innovation for Defence Excellence category, during the Indian Army IDEX Challenge 2020. The award entails a funding of up to INR 15 million.

Creating India's largest private network of soldiers and spouses by Brisk Olive Business Solutions Pvt. Ltd. As of May 2020, the network has over 23,000 members online and over 100,000 offline members. Our Soldier2ndLife initiative is newsworthy and has been featured in national visual and print media.

Advice for the Mad Vets

Be mad! If you are not called "Mad!" at some point in your life, then maybe you have yet to do something new or path breaking!

It does not matter whether you succeed or fail. What matters, *to you*, is to be able to honestly say to yourself, "I gave it my best shot!"

Provide value. Value is all that remains. Unlike you, it does not die. It gets built upon, by another brick in the wall, like you.

Galvanise Mad Vets in Larger Numbers in Nation Building

My way of doing it is through Brisk Olive Business Solutions Pvt. Ltd. Through this, I help soldiers connect together and do great stuff.

Soldiers understand one another and bond instantly. No one has this to the degree to which a soldier has. So a soldier is blessed. Why not use this unique network to build great things?

Options for the Mad Vets to Undertake New Ventures

Soldiers are multi-faceted people. So the range of products and services which they understand, and where they can provide value, is immense. They would perform exceedingly well as:

➢ Trainers and teachers, including trainers of trainers

➢ Product and service providers. Because we are very good at operations and what we like to sell is usually quality

➢ New age ventures, because soldiers understand innovation. And if they can understand the fundamentals of, sales, marketing and finance, nobody can stop them

The Future of India

We are living in the most exciting of times in India. Today, in India, anyone can be anything they want. No longer are they held back by caste, creed, education and money. Well, many still are, but I am talking in the general sense. Today, as an Indian, our limits are set by our imagination and by how we use our inherent huge capabilities.

The writing is on the wall. India is on the way to being a super power in our world. One only hopes that it will be a different kind of super power, not one that is just powerful, but also one that is compassionate and inclusive. And one that strives for quality and fulfilment in the life of its citizens, not just material quantity.

One Mantra for the Mad Vets

Feel happy whenever someone calls you crazy.

That said, be ready to unlearn and learn the rules of the game in the "civil" (non-military) entrepreneurial world. It is an ocean. Once you decide upon something, then go out and learn everything about it. Especially as an entrepreneur, master sales, marketing, the order-to-delivery process, finances and collections. Without these, your business will either not survive or not flourish.

Willingness to Mentor Mad Vets

Certainly. I already mentor some Mad Vets. And I would be happy to mentor more.

On Role of Your Spouse and Parents

Archana Prem is truly my *ardhangini* (one half of me) and the better and less mad part of it. Coming from a defence forces family herself, she probably married an army man for life and rued his changing over to the civil world half way through life. But she took each change in her stride.

I credit the success of both my children, who are extremely successful and happy individuals, to Archana. She has always been there for them, while I was not, most of the time. I made my army profession, my job(s) and my business(es) my purpose, at different stages of my life. And through those, created the best that I could for my wife and children. On the other hand, for her, my success and wellbeing and the wellbeing of our children is her purpose. Undoubtedly, this means giving up many of her own dreams. But never once has she complained or been unhappy about it. On the other hand, she is the one who, whenever things were not looking too good, always said, "Never mind. We will make it through this too."

Some of Archana's characteristics are super efficiency, an even greater ability to work, a large heart and a limitless reservoir from which to give to others. Whether it is supporting someone in their education or just distributing cupcakes to guards, vegetable vendors, children, etc., she is always giving something. And which is why, if ever in need, she will never feel dearth of people ready to help her!

Archana is a home baker. In this, too, she follows her heart. In her own words, she used to get a prize of INR 5 when she cooked at home as a child. And that love for cooking, especially baking, has lasted a lifetime. She never has a dearth of orders, but has not increased her business beyond what she can handle alone. The reasons:

➢ "I enjoy it like this, creating lovely cakes with my own hands. Who knows, as a hard-core businesswoman, maybe I will not enjoy it any longer" and

➢ "Besides, one mad business person in the family is enough!"

To his parents, Sunil credits everything. Says he, "Our parents guided my brother and I, yet they never micro-managed us. They never passed on their limitations and prejudices to us, which I think is extremely important in raising children. I credit all my successes to them. They never posed themselves as role models to us and always trusted and helped us test our own limits and capabilities. Which is why they are my role models!"

* * *

Social Development Activist and Entrepreneur

"Changing mindsets is a much more powerful and permanent means of bringing about integration."

- Colonel Christopher John Rego

Author of *Kovalam and Trivandrum, A Guide Book,* published in 2008, featuring Kovalam, Trivandrum, Poovar and Chowara in Kerala.

Author of *The History of St Joseph's Boys' High School, Bangalore, 1858-2008* published in 2008.

Author of *Cradle of Valour,* a glorious history of the Regimental Centre of the Bombay Sappers, published in a closed publication in 2013.

CEO and Managing Director of Sunbird Trust, conceptualised by him, and registered in 2014 as an NGO engaged in building peace through education in conflict-affected areas of North East India.

Awardee of the International Ashoka Fellowship from South Asia in the year 2016, akin to a worldwide gold standard for early-stage social entrepreneurs.

Trained pianist and proficient in multiple musical instruments including guitar, harmonica, and flute.

Amateur herpetologist, ornithologist, nature lover, photographer, and avid explorer of the wilds of the North East.

Colonel Christopher John Rego is all of the above. He is known as Chris to his family and friends, 'Sir Chris' to the hundreds of sponsored students of Sunbird Trust and their families, and a Gallivanter par excellence from 268 Engineer Bridge Regiment.

Early Life

Chris, the eldest of four siblings, was born in the year 1962 into the illustrious family of Air Commodore Melville Christopher Rego, Indian Air Force. His maternal great grandfather was a Lieutenant Colonel in Royal Indian Medical Department of the British Indian Army during World War I. His maternal grandfather, who had served in Burma during World War II in the Royal Army Medical Corps of the British Indian Army, was also part of the Allied Occupation Force in Japan, and retired as a Major. The family hailed from Bangalore.

Chris did almost his entire schooling at St Joseph Boys' High School, Bangalore, which was quite unique for an armed forces child. His response to this observation showed an unexpected facet of service life. "All four of us siblings were born within a relatively short span of five years, from 1962 to 1966. Our parents were finding it difficult to raise four small children along with frequent transfers which were part of service life. So with great reluctance I was handed over into the care of my maternal grandparents, who lived in a sprawling colonial bungalow in Bangalore. My grandfather was an avid garden lover, and it is from him that I imbibed my love for nature. Both my grandparents and parents gave much of their time to the underprivileged, and it was from them that I developed a deep empathy for the downtrodden in society."

After completing schooling, Chris, with his love for the outdoors, commenced a degree in Agriculture Sciences at University of Agriculture Sciences, Bangalore. The family elders became concerned enough at Chris not following the family tradition of service in the armed forces and convinced him to successfully appear for NDA entrance examinations.

Life in the Army

Chris was unable to meet the eyesight requirement of the IAF and so joined NDA as an Army Cadet in 1980. An average performer in professional subjects, his skills as a musician soon made him very popular amongst his peers. In fact, being the only skilled pianist he was frequently asked to play the grand piano for important occasions in the NDA. Later while at the Indian Military Academy, Chris, a crack shot with the rifle and keen outdoor man, was keen to join the Paratroopers. The Bombay Sappers was the only engineer group assigned the role to provide troops for the Paratroop Field Company. When the time came for Chris to fill up his choice of Arms/Corps, he opted for and was commissioned into the Bombay Sappers in June 1984.

On commissioning, he was posted to 268 Engineer Bridge Unit, then a specialised PMP bridging unit located at Chandimandir, near Chandigarh. Here, he quickly became an expert in field engineering and bridging techniques and made a mark in trials of new equipment. A good sportsman, he captained the Brigade and Corps Troops basketball teams. The unit was frequently in the deserts of Rajasthan on specialised training. Chris was quite happy in this environment, as he enjoyed the time it gave him to master the bridging equipment and also the quality time he got with the troops. He delved into the personal stories of each of his "boys" and this imbibed him with a deep connect with the troops. On the sidelines, it gave him the opportunity to be with nature and pursue his interests. He soon developed camaraderie with the desert shepherds who acquainted him with desert lore and taught him to play the flute. Says Chris, "My stay in the desert camps promoted a sense of enquiry and an urge to explore within me. To see what lay beyond each dune would take me out on lone treks. I learnt to identify the desert flora and fauna including the call of the wolves and the varieties of snakes, deer and other wild life. My shepherd friends became my guides in my quest for knowledge of the desert environment. It no longer looked to me dry and featureless but a vibrant landscape filled with natural wonders and life, albeit of a different genre."

While at Chandimandir, Chris was detailed as an engineer representative on a long range operational patrol in the high-altitude border areas of Himachal Pradesh. The patrol route lay along passes with altitude above 17000 ft. This provided him with an invaluable opportunity to enjoy being an infantryman through the acclimatisation process and the patrol itself. From his patrol mates, the ITBP guides and the local villagers, he sought wisdom of the mountains. He was astonished to encounter polyandry in some of the hill tribes. The month long patrol in the pristine beauty of the pine forests and later the barren snow-covered mountains was for the duration of approximately a month during which he gained much knowledge of the flora and fauna and the customs and traditions of the local hill people.

In 1986, he severely injured his back while playing basketball with his troops. This required major surgery and put paid to his dreams of becoming a paratrooper. Shortly thereafter he moved to CME, Pune for his civil engineering degree course from 1989 to 1991. While honing his professional knowledge, this gave him time to engage in his hobbies of music, nature conversation, bird watching and photography. In fact, he and a friend made a near clean sweep of the annual CME photography competition. He associated with a local youth group 'Conservation Crusaders' and on most weekends would join them on forest treks, bird watching, Nala bunding and tree plantation drives. In the land of Shivaji, Chris and his friends trekked to several of Shivaji's forts.

1992 holds special significance for Chris, as this was the year when he was introduced to his life partner Myrna Pais, like him from a Mangalorean Catholic family, and daughter of an Army Colonel. They held similar passions like a love for nature and music and soon got married. Chris attributes her sacrifice and complete support and encouragement for their success as a family.

Deolali is a quaint little town located in serene and picturesque surroundings. It houses and survives on the School of Artillery. Chris was posted here as the Garrison Engineer in 1992. During his first inspection of his office, his attention fell on long rows of documents in dusty cupboards. The staff apprised him that these were old documents. Out of curiosity, he perused some of them. Thus began his tryst with authorship. The cupboards were a treasure trove of documents tracing back to the start of Deolali cantonment in the 1870s, with drawings for the very first buildings and their construction details. His interest was aroused, and he decided to try and write the history of the cantonment. He was soon joined by Brig Jayant, a retired Artillery officer in the station. As the evolution of the cantonment became clear, they both took time off to visit the Maharashtra State and National Archives at Mumbai.

Chris shares some interesting snippets discovered in his search, "In the aftermath of the first war of independence, British troops were poured into India. As there was no Suez Canal at the time, they arrived at Mumbai after a prolonged sea voyage from England via the Cape of South Africa. For them to rest, recoup and get documented and kitted for their stay in India, a search was made for a cool place close to Mumbai that would serve as a depot. This resulted in the camp at Deolali being set up as a rest and recreation centre for British troops. Later, during World War II, large numbers of wounded British troops needed convalescent facilities prior to repatriation to England. The surgical cases were dispatched to Kirkee, and the medical cases were sent to Ahmednagar. The psychiatric cases were evacuated to Deolali, resulting in coining of British Army slang 'going doolali' indicating that someone was going insane. Further, at the end of their stay in India, soldiers called 'time expired soldiers' came to Deolali for their discharge procedure and preparation to return to England. These were termed as 'time expired soldiers' in British Army slang." After their meticulous research, a book called the *History of Deolali* was authored by Brig Jayant. In the preface, he gave major credit to Chris for his contribution.

In his spare time, Chris often gallivanted around Deolali. He continued his hobby to explore the local forts, one of which was at the Deolali artillery firing range. During one such lone trip, he slipped from the top of the feature on which the fort was and sustained severe injuries all over his body. He found himself lying on a ledge overlooking a steep precipice. Blinding pain coursed through his body on even the slightest movement. There was a long way to go to get to the bottom of the hill. Night was setting in, and the next day there was a planned artillery shoot even as he lay like a stool pigeon on the target. His thoughts strayed to Myrna and his young son who were then at her hometown of Mangalore. His will to live strengthened, and his sub-consciousness tapped into the tremendous source of energy which lies buried deep within the human body. In desperation, Chris crawled and hobbled over a distance of eleven kilometres during the pitch-dark night, before he could be rescued. At the Military Hospital, it took great convincing for the doctors to accept that Chris had trekked eleven kilometres with a compressed vertebrae. This superhuman feat of survival reflected the enormous inner strength of Chris. Though he recovered in time, he was downgraded to a permanent low medical category.

1993 was the year of the great Latur earthquake in Maharashtra. Chris had recovered from his spinal injury and was again at Pune doing another technical course. Recalls Chris, "I vividly remember, it was an extended weekend because of holidays. On getting to know of the extent of the disaster, I just picked up my bag and proceeded to Killari village, the epicentre of the earthquake, by bus. The destruction was unbelievable. Stench from dead bodies was all pervasive. Someone had brought an ambulance, and I befriended the driver. In the day we used it to ferry dead bodies and at night we slept within it. With the dead everywhere, doors and windows of the destroyed houses were used to burn the bodies. I was aghast to see that even in the midst of such death and destruction, the caste consideration of the survivors complicated the search and rescue efforts. The relief effort by the government agencies were stymied by their self-created procedural bottlenecks in the initial period. It was the citizen bodies and private organisations which were in the forefront. I learnt at first hand the requirement of managing relief resources and material which could make a difference to the survivors in the critical first forty-eight hours."

After Deolali, Chris spent the next few years with his unit 268 ENGINEERS. They have the capability to span wet gaps of up to couple of hundred metres. The bridges are designed to provide crossing to the heaviest main battle tanks of the armed forces. Before launching the bridges, bank slopes and the water flow have to be reconnoitred to identify the possible bridging sites, approaches to the sites have to be prepared for moving of the heavy equipment, and simultaneously enemy mines have to be cleared. But the most difficult part is accomplishing the above tasks in pitch darkness, under enemy fire and all this while maintaining complete secrecy of the bridging operation. Discovery by the enemy would inevitably invite the heaviest artillery and air strikes. The entire operation is extremely difficult and time sensitive and has to be accomplished in the shortest possible time frame of one to three hours duration, depending on the technical difficulties on site. Continuous and rigorous practice is essential to enable the construction parties to work with clockwork precision to fit the bridge components.

Recalls Chris, now a Company Commander with the unit, "We were part of a major exercise in the desert during peak of winters. It was midnight, and temperature hovered near freezing point. The bridging operations were underway and suddenly a situation arose. Two of the pontoons got stuck due to the fast water current, and the connecting pins could not be joined despite desperate efforts of the men. Launching the bridge in time was most critical to the success of the entire operation. I began to receive frantic calls from the Commanding Officer who was at another site. As the Company Commander, I immediately jumped into the freezing canal to join my men. Seeing me in the water with them gave them a new energy, and shouting the regimental battle cry '268 Sarvashresth' and with superhuman strength, we manoeuvred the pontoons into place. We were all wet, exhausted and shivering with cold. Suddenly we sensed ground vibrations under our feet and a thundering crescendo of sound enveloped the bridging site. It seemed to emanate from all the cardinal directions of the horizon. We forgot our physical discomfort. With the launch of our bridge successful, the leading Combat

Groups of the famed Indian Strike Corps were already homing onto the bridge, in a finely orchestrated manoeuver, to carry the battle deep into 'enemy' territory. The satisfaction of we being the leading elements in setting the stage for the commencement of deep battle and witness from closest quarters the awe-inspiring spectacle of the armoured fighting vehicles with battened down hatches, crossing over our bridges in pitch darkness, never ceases to inspire me. It still gives me goose bumps on the skin."

One of the most prestigious individual competitions organised by the Corps of Engineers is the Annual Bewoor Essay competition. With his deep professional knowledge, Chris became the proud winner of this competition in 1997. Despite his professional competency, his medical handicap became a major stumbling block in his career advancement. Chris took it in his stride and opted to skill himself in lateral avenues.

In 2001 Chris opted for a two-year study leave to pursue Masters in Business Management in HR and Marketing at Xavier Institute of Management & Entrepreneurship, Bangalore. It was customary for the students to themselves select two class prefects. Despite a two-decade age gap between Chris and fellow students, they fell under his magic spell, and he was unanimously voted as the first choice for the class prefect during both his years at the institute! He also innovatively introduced the army buddy system in studies and became the first from the institute to secure an international internship for two months at Singapore Stock Exchange. Chris organised several educational trips to local IT and Business ventures. He was placed in charge of the Socially Useful and Productive Activities of the institute and took his batchmates out on blood donation drives, visiting the elderly at homes for the aged and spending time with children at juvenile delinquent centres. On the day of graduation, he was presented with the award of 'Graduate with the Best Potential Value to Society.'

On close of his study leave, Chris opted for a tenure in the North East. He received his posting to Assam Rifles at Shillong, Meghalaya but was soon side stepped to Aizawl, Mizoram. This proved to be a turning point in his life as it was here that he found his second calling for working for peace and national integration.

Though the Mizo Peace accord had been signed in 1986 and the situation had improved substantially, the hangover of the militancy days was still palpable in the environment. Much of the populace were still weighed down by the baggage of the past and maintained an antipathy to the Indian state and their countrymen from the 'mainland.' A social divide appeared to exist between the army personnel and the local population, further exacerbated by cultural differences.

Chris and his wife Myrna took a conscious decision to make personal attempts to bridge this divide. They befriended the local citizens they came into contact with and frequently invited them home in the Assam Rifles campus for music sessions. Their local friends were in turn warm hosts treating the Regos to delectable Mizo cuisine. The Regos and their children heartily participated in local festivals and called their friends over to celebrate Diwali, something that these folks had never done before. The Rego children made many Mizo friends with whom they are in contact till today. The family also attended the Mizo church services on Sundays.

Noticing the rapport of Chris with the local community, the Sector Commander informally tasked him to explore reasons for the angst that still existed in the local community against the state. The community elders opened up to Chris. While many appreciated the role of the army in maintaining the peace, a few of them felt the army and Assam Rifles were standoffish, looked down upon the locals, kept aloof from celebrating their festivals and sometimes ill-treated them at security checkposts. Seeing Chris's recommendations, the Sector Commander decided to implement them. That Christmas, he asked Chris to make it a Christmas like never before. Chris and Myrna got near life-size statues of an entire Nativity Scene crafted from Bengali artisans near Silchar. This giant crib, of a size never seen before at Mizoram, was inaugurated at a prominent place at Aizawl under the banner of the Assam Rifles. Thousands of Mizos witnessed this amazing spectacle that was repeated year after year. Additionally, posts of the Assam Rifles across the state went the extra mile to prominently light up their campuses during the Christmas season. Quite expectedly, seeing the Assam Rifles lustily participating in their own festivals, the mindset of local people began to change.

Chris travelled extensively through the length and breadth of Mizoram on official tours of duty. His primary objective as the Engineer Officer of the Sector was to improve the accommodation and comfort of the troops, and he did this to the immense satisfaction of the Sector Commander. During his travels, he learnt that the lack of access to educational facilities was a major issue with the local communities. Chris and Myrna became seized with the issue and the idea of 'being the change' for social development began to take shape. Chris is passionate in saying, "We started out with sponsoring the education of some of the local children from our personal funds. Soon, family and friends were motivated and began contributing to the cause. From the initial lot of our sponsored children, some of whom were already in professional courses, one is now a super specialist doctor and another, from a Chakma refugee family, is an accomplished lawyer. Both are now Advisors with our Trust."

Chris continues, "With our developed love for all things Mizo, Myrna and I started enjoying Mizo gastronomy in all its simplicity sans the masalas and the spices. During my many duty trips to remote areas across the state, I made detailed notes of Mizo cuisine, even venturing into the forest and the fields to learn about the various ingredients. Myrna too had cookery classes from her Mizo friends. Together, we penned down our collection of more than 60 Mizo recipes. Our combined effort, thereafter, constituted the entire chapter on Mizo cuisine in the book *NE Belly*, featuring recipes of North East India by Ashish Chopra."

Chris continues, "My travels across Mizoram on duty gave me a great opportunity to practice my hobby of photography. The Department of Information and Publicity at Aizawl became seized of the photographs I had taken and published many of them in the information brochures of the state."

In 2006, Chris' tenure with the Assam Rifles at Aizawl was coming to an end. He realised that year was the 20th anniversary of the Mizo Peace Accord and mooted the idea of a big celebration with his Mizo friends. Together they drew up a plan that was quickly adopted by the State Government. Chris and Myrna saw this as an excellent opportunity to project the goodwill of the armed forces by them joining a public celebration of a landmark event. The celebration was a massive success with an extravaganza of cultural events and musical performances with full participation of the government and the townsfolk. Importantly, the Assam Rifles were a big part of the celebrations with their jazz band regaling the crowds with Bollywood numbers. The icing on the cake was an Air Force helicopter dropping flowers over the crowd.

Chris mentions, "With our most enjoyable and eventful stay in Mizoram, Myrna and I were convinced that this would be the beginning of our lifelong association with the people of the North East. The nascent thoughts would a few years down the line crystalise into Sunbird Trust."

After his life-changing tenure in the North East, Chris was posted in 2006, with the Air Force Training Command at Bangalore as a Staff Officer in the Engineering section. Here, he helped strategise the new projects and maintenance budget of the Command and contributed immensely to updating various procedures. The fact of St Joseph Boys' High School being a half-hour drive away provided him with ample opportunity to interact with his alma mater. It was but natural for his son to be admitted to this school, as the fourth generation student from the family. Chris acknowledged the role played by the school in the life of his family and in nurturing social values by authoring a 350-page book *The History of St. Joseph's Boys' High School, 1858 – 2008,* which recorded the 150 years of the school's history. The book was released on the 150th anniversary of the school in September 2008 by fellow alumnus and cricketer Rahul Dravid. Chris is proud that his book contains among the last illustrations sketched by the renowned cartoonist and illustrator, Padma Bhushan, late Mario Miranda, also an alumnus of the school.

During his tenure at Bangalore, at the request of a friend who owned a publishing company, Chris was the writer for a detailed travelogue *Kovalam and Trivandrum, A Guide Book,* featuring the beach town of Kovalam along with Trivandrum and the tourist resorts of Poovar and Chowara.

In 2009, Chris was posted to BEG Centre, Pune. His interests were by now widely known. BEG Centre has a sprawling campus teeming with bird and reptile life. Chris began getting frequent calls for 'rescuing snakes and humans from each other!' This earned him the sobriquet of 'Sapera' – a snake charmer.

The Corps of Engineers has three groups. The Bengal Sappers at Roorkee in Uttarakhand, Bombay Sappers at Pune, Maharashtra and Madras Sappers at Bangalore, Karnataka. The East India Company, as part of its governance structure in India, had set up three Presidencies during the second half of the seventeenth century at Madras, Bombay and Calcutta. Separate engineering support components were set up for each of these Presidencies. Over a period of time they evolved into Bombay Sappers, Madras Sappers and Bengal Sappers. While the Madras and Bengal Sappers had detailed archives, Bombay Sappers was almost devoid of any historical records, especially for the 1800s. Quite naturally, with Chris' contribution to the history of Deolali and his book on his school, he was an obvious candidate to research the history of the Centre. The Bombay Sappers hierarchy informally assigned Chris this important task. The book *Cradle of Valour* was the result of two years of his toils and was released by the COAS in 2013.

Says Chris, "With my experience of researching the history of Deolali, I scoured the National Archives at Bombay and online archives on the internet. My research took me through 15,000 pages of old documents. In the process I was also able to discover the reason for the absence of historical records of Bombay Sappers. It was a reference to a mention in 1895 in the notes of the then Commandant of the BEG Centre about an 'Economical Subaltern.' Apparently, the then Commandant had tasked a young Subaltern to 'take the boys out for firing.' The Subaltern in turn tasked a Subedar for making the necessary administrative arrangements. When the Subedar reverted with the input about non-availability of target paper for the firing party, the young Subaltern advised 'jugaad karo' (innovate). The Subedar commandeered old office papers lying haphazardly in a decrepit store room in the office complex. These were turned into target paper and shot to pieces. What remained was burnt. Thus all records of the Bombay Sappers at the Centre dating from the late 18th century to late 19th century were sacrificed at the altar of expediency."

By the time his tenure at BEG Centre was drawing to a close, Chris became due for his last leg posting in anticipation of his superannuation in 2016. The officer's request for last leg posting is generally given due weightage to assist in post-retirement settling down. However, Chris surprised his controlling directorate at Army Headquarters by requesting a posting to insurgency-affected Manipur in the North East. The incredulous officer was bewildered by this unexpected request of Chris. Nevertheless, he obliged, and in July 2012 Chris was posted as Officer Commanding to a BRO unit in Imphal, Manipur. At that time, he was the only army officer posted with the BRO at Imphal.

Change of Uniform

It is difficult to draw a distinctive line defining the fading away of 'Colonel Chris' and rise of 'Chris Sir.' But looked at holistically, the posting to Manipur may be defined as the watershed between the swan song of 'Colonel Chris' and the rise of 'Chris Sir.' It became one of the most energetic, invigorating and accomplished tenures of Chris. The days were spent in extensive tours of duty to remote Border Roads detachments and the evenings were busy in planning the contours of his post-retirement passion.

The North East is prone to rise of centrifugal forces from time to time. Tensions flow from Centre-State disputes, conflicts between indigenous tribes and cultures, fear of unfavourable demographic imbalance by settling of migrants from other parts of the country and illegal immigrants. Some of the major groups which exercise considerable influence amongst the people at large are United Liberation Front of Assam (ULFA) and National Democratic Front of Bodoland (NDFB) in Assam, Garo National Liberation Army (GNLA) in Meghalaya, National Liberation Front of Tripura (NLFT) in Tripura, Mizo National Front (MNF) in Mizoram, United National Liberation front (UNLF) and National Socialist Council of Nagaland (NSCN) in both Nagaland and Manipur and (People's Liberation Army) PLA in Manipur. Arunachal Pradesh is the only state largely devoid of militancy. For the better part, the terrain is hilly, thickly forested, sparsely populated and with very few roads and tracks, making it favourable topography for operations of militant groups.

Adds Chris, "Few people understand that historically, for the Naga tribes, the village was their nation state. There have been instances in the not too distant past where even people of same the tribe but hailing from different villages have paid the price of transgressing village boundaries with their lives. With such strong nationalist fervour, it was but natural to resist the authority of the Indian state. In Manipur, prior to the 18th century the original religion of the Meities of Manipur was Sanamahi, an animistic religion involving worship of ancestors, wind, sun and fire, etc. It was during the reign of their King Gharaib Nawas, in early 18th century that they converted enmasse to Vaishnavite Hinduism. They have a very rich culture with highly evolved literature, dance and art forms. Ethnically, culturally, psychologically and emotionally many espouse greater affinity with the South East Asian culture than to mainland India."

Chris was posted with BRO, with an overwhelming civilian staff and workforce. BRO personnel do not carry weapons on duty and were very often at the coercive end of militant actions. Extortion demands, maltreatment of BRO drivers especially after minor accidents, threatening of migrant labourers from Bihar and even occasional IED blasts were a part of work. Being the only army officer with the organisation at Imphal, and though not in his charter of duties, Chris was the point person to deal with all such situations, many of them life threatening. This required a different form of cold courage where he had to walk in alone, unarmed, with his force of personality as the only backup.

On several occasions, he escaped death by the proverbial whisker, when arraigned before the court of village elders, with shadowy armed men lounging in the background to execute the decision of the tribal court. More than a dozen BRO personnel are alive today because Chris refused to be coerced and dared to defend them. Chris simply says, "I was just following the Chetwood motto immortalised at IMA. Safety of my subordinates is my prime concern."

Despite the massive risks BRO officers and personnel took in their daily work, to add insult to the injury, the Controller of Defence Accounts Officers (CDA O) arbitrarily refused to admit his claim for grant of Special Compensatory Counter Insurgency Allowance stating that personnel on deputation with BRO could not be entitled to the allowance. It took an RTI application and filing a suit at the Armed Forces Tribunal to get redress. The position of the CDA O was on such flimsy grounds, that the decision in favour was awarded in the very first hearing with costs and substantial damages. This ruling not only benefitted Chris, but also many army colleagues serving in Manipur and Nagaland as well.

His personal interest in getting to know the true reality of the people and the region involved great personal risk to himself. It was under these challenging circumstances that the opportunity he was seeking emerged. Chris reminisces, "A group of Naga people walked into my office. They were from Village Ijeirong, an idyllic hamlet in verdant forests about three hours' drive from Imphal. They had heard about my work and had come to seek assistance for setting up infrastructure for their village school. The entire area had a presence of the NSCN (IM). I took a leap of faith and drove to the village, traversing a long stretch of thickly forested terrain without any protection. I fell in love with the village and its hospitable inhabitants at first sight. Children from a cluster of seven to eight villages came to study in the school, which was a collection of ramshackle tin sheds. Since the villages were spaced far apart, children, some as young as 7 years old, stayed on rent in the huts of local families and managed their daily life as 'self-help children.' This meant that they independently cooked, washed and cleaned and managed to study as well. With the parents leaving bags of rice and stacks of firewood, these children augmented their rations by scrounging in the forest for edible leaves, roots and mushrooms. The village had no electricity."

Chris continues, "I liaised with the BRO and Assam Rifles, who magnanimously provided constructional material for bare essentials. The villagers provided the work force, and under my guidance a hostel was constructed within six months. With the formation of Sunbird Trust later that year, supporting paraphernalia like solar lighting, kitchens and water supply were provided. This became the first building of educational infrastructure for Sunbird Trust."

Colonel Christopher John Rego hung his uniform on 31 January 2016. The very next day, on 1st February, Chris assumed the duties of CEO of Sunbird Trust.

Sunbird Trust

It is difficult to comprehend a man making it his life's mission to work amongst a population from which militants emerged to shoot and kill who they perceived as their enemies, soldiers included. Chris is categorical in his response, "During the course of my prolonged and deep interaction with people in North East India, I had full trust in their humanism and developed a strong bond with them. The people from the rural interiors were an inspiration with how happy they were with their simple lives without materialistic yearnings. Most were subsistence farmers who eked out a living from their small landholdings or the forest. Their lives were devoid of the luxuries of modern civic infrastructure. At several places, there were no roads, electricity or water supply. Yet, they made the best of what nature had to offer. They had deep family bonds, a strong sense of community and much civic sense. I could not but empathise with them. While as a soldier with a gun in hand, I had a duty to my country, even to shoot to kill in worst circumstances in safeguarding the nation's interests. That was the oath I had taken. Post retirement I am still serving my country, albeit in a different form. Through my organisation I am now engaged in changing mindsets, a much more powerful and permanent means of bringing about integration of people and fostering peace. Their aspirations are really simple to meet. Food on the table, security for the family, education and employment for their children. When we pull the children into the net of education, we are empowering them and giving them employability and the opportunity to make better choices in their lives. This empowerment would certainly wean them away from the financial compulsions and traditional mindsets that fuel insurgency. Their education would provide them escape from the frog-in-the-well outlook and provide them with a window to the world and the opportunities in the rest of India."

Sunbird Trust is the brainchild of Chris. Service constraints restricted him from forming any organisation while in uniform. However, his strong ideas for fostering peace through the means of education had by then influenced many of his friends. In preparation for Chris's retirement barely 14 months later, two of them registered Sunbird Trust on 11 December 2020 and became its trustees. Chris had no role in the organisation till he took over as CEO. At Sunbird, with full transparency, the trustees are the apex decision-making body and sole authority to approve any financial expenditure. They are guided by a Board of Advisors with six members who are eminent citizens.

After Sunbird Trust's partnership with the Ijeirong village school, called Paangkriang Friendship School (PFS), and its vastly improved infrastructure, the number of its students grew by leaps and bounds. Between 2016 and 2019, the school had grown from about 100 students to 450, all of who came from neighbouring villages. The hostel itself, appropriately named 'Sunbird Friendship Hostel,' started with forty students in the first year, had 250 students by 2019. As most were from families of subsistence farmers, Sunbird Trust contributed majorly to sponsoring the school and hostel children and also supporting the salaries of the teachers. To keep their skin in the game, the parents were expected to pay nominal fees to support the operational expenditure of the school. So, for instance, at the hostel, while the expenditure of each child was about Rs 1,200, Sunbird Trust contributed Rs 650 and the parents paid Rs 300, with the rest being contributed in rice for their own children. Even those who were too poor paid a fraction of the fees in terms of firewood or rice for the hostel.

The story of Sunbird Trust and its partnership with the PFS in a remote village in Manipur soon spread far and wide. By now, many interns, especially Teach for India Fellows, had started coming for short stints during their leave. This was also the time when a 23-year-old woman hailing from Kerala became the first to apply to join the Trust. Aswathy Jayakumar, a graduate from BITS, Pilani had just completed a two-year fellowship with 'Teach for India,' a Bombay-based NGO. Chris was uncertain about recruiting her, as Sunbird Trust did not pay salaries and for a young woman to stay in a remote village with few amenities was quite a challenge. Aswathy, however, persisted and became the first 'outsider' to live in the village. She was one of the key influencers in changing the mindsets of local people towards the 'outsiders.' As a trained teacher, she set up the curriculum and pedagogy of the school and the other schools that Sunbird Trust had begun to partner with.

By now the impact of Sunbird Trust had started emerging, and many persons visited the school. The word spread, and for the first time, Sunbird Trust started receiving donations. The Trust had adhered to all legal compliances and was able to offer the 80G tax concession to its donors. Today PFS is now well on its way to becoming a model school. The entire campus is equipped with solar power, an 18 terminal computer lab, a science laboratory, music academy, two hostels with 250 beds and two playfields. Additionally, Ijeirong is the "Field Headquarters" of

Sunbird Trust with staff accommodation and a fully equipped Sunbird Centre. Three highly trained and committed Sunbird Team members stay at Ijeirong, helping administer the school and improve the education standards. All other partner schools of Sunbird Trust are being upgraded along the same lines.

Sunbird Trust promotes access to education in two ways. The first is by helping build and run schools and hostels. The second is by sponsoring education of students from economically weak families in Sunbird Trust schools and partner schools across the North East. The Trust activities are spread over the states of Manipur, Assam, Nagaland and Arunachal Pradesh.

Chris recounts, "Today we are partnering with fifty-three schools and institutions, fully or partly sponsoring the education of 3,300 students. We have also built or are building fifteen schools and hostels in collaboration with our local partners. Twenty young professionals from all across the country constitute the Sunbird Trust team. Most live and work at our Sunbird partner institutions in the North East. Sunbird Trust's COO is a former intern, Dr Sonal Sethia, Post Graduate in Biotechnology from IIT Mumbai and PhD from University of Glasgow. The others include Teach for India Fellows, MBAs, engineers and other professionals. Chris says, "As a matter of our core ideology, we are a humanistic, non-sectarian and non-religious organisation that does not promote any religious or political agenda. In fact, given my personal background of four generations in uniform, we seek to promote acceptance of plurality and diversity. This is amply reflected in our Sunbird Team which has people of five religions from different parts of the country. We follow the motto of 'Deepen your roots and broaden your vision' whereby we encourage our children to celebrate their own culture, but at the same time to appreciate the culture of others."

On being asked about the future expansion of the Trust activities and sourcing of funds, Chris says, "Sunbird Trust's vision 2025 is to build 50 institutions, schools or hostels, and sponsor the education of

25,000 children. As of now, we are well on track, but will have to be wary of the effects of the COVID crisis. Myrna and I are parenting 35 students from the North Eastern states at Bangalore and Kolar, who are studying for their engineering, law, Bachelor of Arts and Bachelor of Science degrees. Their expenditure is being sponsored by the Trust. We look to increasing these numbers substantially and empowering many, many more youngsters from the North East. We have started a Sunbird Fellowship with the objective of training and absorbing local talent into the organisation. We have three members now and hope to progressively increase it to hundred persons. Since education is not a silver bullet and panacea for solving all social problems, we are also planning to expand into livelihood-generating activities such as eco-tourism, mushroom farming, Roselle tea manufacturing and mud oven bakery produce. For funds, we are dependent on committed institutional donors and individuals. Our name has spread abroad as well, and we have many supporters among NRI and Overseas Citizens of India. We have applied for permission to accept foreign funds and are hopeful of getting the same. Sunbird has applications from young professionals from across India to join us in our work. As each 'outsider' is a powerful agent of integration, we want it to become a movement. "

Sunbird Trust team members are undeterred by the last vestiges of the militancy in the areas where they work. Given that Sunbird provides the best opportunity for education and empowerment of the children, the mothers of the village are their security and even the militants dare not go against the wishes of these womenfolk. Well-meaning benefactors from the rest of India are coming forward in large numbers to sponsor higher education of these children in mainland institutions. This itself has a huge integrating effect on the mindset of the parents. Background support by the army and Assam Rifles has opened new lines of communication between the state apparatus and the population. New hope is dawning in the North East as it forsakes its violent past and reaps the dividend of peace.

CHRISTOPHER SPEAKS

Learnings from the Army

Learnt to celebrate and profit from the diversity and plurality of our country.

Realised the true meaning of loyalty to humanity, to country, to team and to fellow citizens; to transcend narrow parochial allegiances.

Imbibed deep sense of intellectual, moral and physical courage.

Value of team work in planning and building organisational capabilities.

Philosophy Towards Life

I always look at the abundance around me, rather than scarcity. Power and position is material to be used to help the lesser privileged.

Personal Qualities that Have Helped

Deep sense of enquiry and curiosity.

Trust in goodness of human nature, unless proven otherwise.

Deep-rooted love for nature has always assisted me in maintaining a positive outlook towards life.

Out-of-the-box thinking.

Tenacity in pursuit of my goals.

Difficulties and Overcoming Them

The spinal injuries sustained by me were serious enough to restrict me from leading a far more active life. But I employed my inner mental strength to overcome them, and I now lead an energetic and vigorous life. It is the same inner strength which enabled me to move eleven kilometres with a compressed vertebra and injured back.

The biggest challenge faced by us was the physical safety of our lives, as we worked in a militancy-prone environment without a shred of protection. It was our people connect and trust established by our dedication that enabled us to overcome this difficulty.

We dreamt big driven by our vision, passion and commitment to our cause. This required resources beyond the means available with us. We worked away from the public eye, in a far corner of the country, deep in the forests. This lack of visibility, in the initial days, impacted our fundraising ability. So we scouted for people and organisations with similar values and vision. It was the power of our networking skills which enabled us to generate adequate resources for the tasks at hand. Today our reputation and work speaks for itself, and it attracts the philanthropists to join us to mutually achieve common goals.

Impacting Life of Others

Our work has set in motion a subtle change in the decades-old mindset of violence and antipathy towards the mainland. This has released the ethnic populace from generations-old angst. The resultant accumulation of negative energy had held back their own development. At the same time, I believe we have given our numerous visitors, interns and donors a mindset change in realising the reality of people from the North East, their strengths, culture and aspirations.

The release from past baggage and access to quality education has opened new avenues of livelihood for a whole new generation in the areas of our operations.

Three Major Achievements of Your Enterprise

Sunbird Trust has been able to create infrastructure for five functional institutions, and is raising another ten, large and small, within just five years of its existence. The achievement is all the more noteworthy given the fact that they are in remote, conflict-impacted locations.

Our next big success has been our ability to attract highly qualified young professionals from across the country into our fold. They have abjured lucrative corporate opportunities to take joy in pursuing their passions with us in remote conflict-ridden regions of the country.

Our four main project centres at Ijeirong, Khomunnom, Puichi and Langmai have become hubs of peace and friendship building, impacting thousands of children, their parents and communities.

My being awarded the prestigious international Ashoka Fellowship from South Asia in 2016 has been one of our greatest recognitions. This recognition came when our organisation was still in its infancy.

Advice for the Mad Vets

You are highly privileged to have wealth of experience, knowledge, administrative ability and ability to work across cultures. Please leverage these assets, as they provide you with a head start which few possess.

Find your true inner calling and passion, and make a plan to realise it. The means will follow automatically. You will do well to follow your passion trail rather than the money trail.

How to Galvanise Mad Vets in Larger Numbers in Nation Building

The Mad Vets have a much stronger sense of the nation than ordinary citizens. Using our position in society to work for the underprivileged, the environment or other social causes is immensely self-satisfying. Creating jobs and helping strengthen bonds between people contributes vastly to nation building.

Options for the Mad Vets to Undertake New Ventures

Leverage your technical competency and professional knowledge. The social sector empowers your higher self. So you can go back to your rural roots to transform your village, your community, your region, where you have much leverage.

Greening wastelands, provisioning solar energy and provisioning quality education in far-flung areas will provide you with a sense of satisfaction and joy. Start small ventures at personal level and grow them.

The Future of India

The youth of India are bursting with unbridled energy. Unshackling of regulatory chains, which were holding back the entrepreneurial minds, will release innovative energy.

These forces are already driving the pace of change in society and economy. India is arriving at its legitimate place in the community of nations when old alliances and businesses are fading.

One Mantra for the Mad Vets

Find your grain of passion and commence the ride. Success shall follow.

Willingness to Mentor Mad Vets

It's always a privilege to hold the hands of a passionate veteran. I am already on this journey by assisting a veteran who is leading the change in his village in Madhya Pradesh, by setting up a quality education institute.

On Role of Your Spouse

Myrna is my life partner in the real sense of the term. She has put in tremendous sacrifice and labour in bringing up our two children and handling so many difficulties while I was away. This is perhaps the single-most important reason for the success and the comfortable position we find ourselves in now.

She is herself a French tutor and teacher of repute. Her strength lies in her deep love for the family and the extended family of Sunbird Trust.

* * *

How the experiences determine the shifts in conscience and understanding

SHADES OF GREY

White is the truth to the innocence of a child,
Lie is black and with evil tis synonymous.
A clear demarcation for ease of interpretation.
Conscience clear and the border well seen,
Right equals truth, wrong is the lie, so easy to define.

Thence emerges the impatience of youth
From which flows the fudging of lines,
Broadening the No Man's Land between white and black.
Whims and fancies rule the divide,
An element of grey is introduced in between.

Body grows but not the mind, the intellect opines,
I am right and you are wrong, what ego determines,
Conscience is the balm that heals resultant harm.
As you vacillate between white right black wrong,
Conscience basks in shades of grey around.
You do right and yet do wrong,
It's all about conscience is the wisdom that dawns.
Here right is grey and wrong too is grey,
Conscience is the key that selects the shade.
Follow the conscience is what the peace of mind demands.
From this determination now flows right and wrong,
The shade of grey that is your truth.
The thought that brings no peace of mind is a lie to you,
Welcome to the shades of grey that are the truth.

- Col RS Sidhu

* * *

Marine Instrumentation and Communication Systems Solution Provider

In business dealings, I have come across three types of people, the Do Gooders, Rule Sticklers and Self-Interest predominant. Idea is to identify the person you are dealing with and read mantra accordingly.

- CPO Radhakrishnan Varier

Linia Engineering Services

Linia Engineering Services, set up in 1996, is a proprietary firm with Master Chief Electrical Artificer (Power) 1st Class Radhakrishnan Varier (Veteran) as the Sole Proprietor. Today with fifty-odd employees on its rolls, offices in Mumbai and Vishakhapatnam, manufacturing unit in Mumbai, the firm has an annual revenue turnover of INR 5 Crores and supplies military grade marine instruments and communication systems for almost the  entire spectrum of IN ships ranging from Patrol Vessels, Landing Ship Tanks, Tankers, Destroyers, Submarines and Aircraft Carriers.

It also has Non-Disclosure Agreements with foreign firms from four countries, Memorandum of Understanding with one foreign firm for manufacturing of its systems and undertakes specified Annual Maintenance Contracts for specialised ships of the IN.

The Proprietor of Linia Engineering Services, Radhakrishnan, was born in 1959 into an orthodox family in the deep interiors of Palakkad district of Kerala. He was the second of three siblings. His father was a government middle school teacher and mother a housewife. Radhakrishnan proved to be a bright student in school and regularly topped his class. His interest lay in engineering, but owing to financial constraints of his family, he could realistically look forward to only a diploma from a Government Polytechnic Institute. By meritorious hard work he was able to secure admission in a Government Polytechnic Institute.

Radhakrishnan would start from his village by seven in the morning to study at the Polytechnic, and it would be seven in the evening by the time he returned home. After six months, his father decided to put him into the campus hostel. Hailing from an orthodox family of a pious school teacher, the cosmopolitan culture of the hostel proved to be a cultural shock to young Radhakrishnan. Christians, Muslims, Hindus, rich, poor, elders, vegetarians and non-vegetarians all stayed together under the same roof and ate at the same table. Clothing and toiletries became a common pool to be utilised on first come basis by the room mates. Radhakrishnan resisted all attempts to induce him to eat non-vegetarian food, but succumbed to smoke his first cigarette.

At the age of 16 years, Radhakrishnan was faced with his first difficult life choice. His father had retired from his job of school teacher and from his meagre monthly pension of INR 500 had to cater for expenditure on studies of his younger brother, now promoted to high school, and for possible marriage of his sister, of marriageable age. There was no money left for Radhakrishnan to pursue his studies any further. So he decided to opt for recruitment into the armed forces, as suggested by his maternal uncle, himself an army man. Accompanied by his cousin and another school teacher, he travelled from Palakkad to Calicut, present-day Kozhikode. This was the first time in his life that he saw the sea. At the Recruitment Office he learnt that there were vacancies only for Navy in Apprentice Entry Scheme and Boys Entry Scheme. Not understanding the nuances, he opted for the latter, a decision he would come to regret later, as this was the lowest possible entry status into the Navy. He did not have to undergo written exams because of his academic grades and easily qualified in physical performance tests. He was now required to report to INS Circar at Vishakhapatnam for joining Naval Boys training. Radhakrishnan also had to forego his first year practical exams for the Polytechnic to join the Naval training in time.

Navy Life

On 4th of July 1975, Radhakrishnan joined INS Circar for Naval Boys training, his first travel outside Kerala. There were approximately 400 trainees in his batch. Bunk bed, crew cut, boots, singlet and deck cap made him homesick. Navy had not been his first choice. The only silver lining for him was the monthly payment of INR 20, out of a total monthly salary of INR 40, which enabled him to partake of 'jalebis and samosas.'

On completion of basic training, Radhakrishnan was assigned Electrical Engineering trade and transferred to INS Valsura, Jamnagar in Gujarat for technical training. There he came across Artificers undergoing training and realised his mistake of not opting for Artificer Entry. To rectify the earlier mistake, he opted to appear for Artificer Entry exams and cleared them. So while his batchmates, on completion of training in 1976, joined as Sailors, Radhakrishnan underwent another four years of training and joined on board a Petya Class Patrol Vessel as Artificer in 1980. In his words, "I thanked my stars for my fortuitous decision to opt for Artificer training when in later service I came across one of my Boys training batchmates as a mess boy while I was an Artificer on board the same ship."

Petya Class Patrol Boats of the IN are roughly 90 metres by 9 metres in dimension. The on board infrastructure for the crew is highly inadequate. There are mere four water closets and three bathing cubicles for a crew of roughly hundred personnel. Sea water is channelled for use in water closets and is freely available. But flow of fresh water in the bathing cubicles is another matter. Extreme measures are the norm to conserve fresh water. "Fresh water for next five minutes" announcement over the ship address system invariably results in a mad scramble for the bathing cubicles. Missing the sacrosanct deadline of five minutes was tantamount to saying goodbye to wash your sweat-encrusted smelling body for the next twenty-four hours. Rushing into the bathing cubicle for wetting the body, rushing out to soap the body and then again rushing in to cleanse the soap from the body, alternating with twenty to thirty other crew members is the norm. Electrical Artificer (Power) Radhakrishnan Varier spent one full decade of his life, from 1980 to 1990, participating in this scramble on board the Petya ships.

Life on board the Petya class ship was tough. Crew infrastructure was rudimentary. With a draught of just three metres, it was sensitive to pitch and yaw motions induced by the ocean waves. So Radhakrishnan was prone to frequent bouts of sea sickness on board the Petya ships. He became mentally robust and resilient. Self-discipline became a second nature to him. He also gained invaluable hands-on experience in every engineering control system during his ten years of service with the Petya Class ships. This experience would later on prove to be the bedrock on which he would successfully build his Linia Engineering Services.

Soon, Radhakrishnan developed aspiration to become an Officer in the Navy through the Commission Worthy Scheme, but failed in his first attempt. Two other colleagues of his went on to clear the examination and subsequently retired as Commodore/Captain. He was unable to appear for the second attempt, as he had to be operated upon for hernia and was downgraded in medical category. Destiny had other plans for him.

During his service with the Navy, he got two opportunities to travel abroad. First was on board a Petya ship on a goodwill visit to Singapore. During the long journey to Singapore, the crew had to perforce stay without a bath for fourteen days, to conserve fresh water. The second time, Radhakrishnan was selected to be part of crew detailed to take over a new naval ship in Russia. So he learnt Russian, to be better able to perform his role. The two visits gave him deep insight into dealing with foreigners.

Radhakrishnan got married in 1987 while posted on board a ship at Vishakhapatnam. Radhakrishnan recalls, "After marriage my wife came to Visakhapatnam, accompanied by her brother. As I had just got married & because of my low seniority, I was not eligible for married accommodation allotted by Navy. I arranged for one room accommodation with one of my friends. So there were three of us living and cooking in the same room. The kitchen was set up, and my wife made preparations to cook her first meal for us. In the meantime, I went to the dockyard where my ship was berthed. Suddenly, we received orders to set sail for Sri Lanka. Operation Pawan, the IPKF operation in Sri Lanka, had commenced. There was no time to say goodbye to my wife. It was two months before we returned and I could taste the first meal from our kitchen."

Changing the Uniform

His contractual service period as Artificer with the Navy was for ten years after the training, that is, up to 1990. At close of contractual service, Radhakrishnan applied for extension of service by another five years. The extension would enable him to plan for life beyond the Navy.

Radhakrishnan analysed all the options available and shortlisted the fields of shipping, government reserved jobs, onshore jobs in foreign countries, jobs within India and own business. He then meticulously went about equipping himself, over the next five years, with academic and technical qualifications for the shortlisted sectors:

➢ Associates Member of Institution of Engineers (India) Examination, equivalent to Bachelors in Engineering Degree
➢ Diploma in Business Management from Indian Merchant Chambers
➢ Six-month Certificate Course in Computers
➢ Certificate from Ministry of Shipping for Merchant Navy

By the time Radhakrishnan was released from service with the Navy on 31 August 1995, on completion of his contractual terms, he had acquired the relevant academic qualifications. As the future post Navy life was uncertain he shifted his family to Palakkad, so as to be free of domestic concerns, to make his way in the rough and tumble of life in the civil street.

A day after being released from the Navy, Radhakrishnan joined as a Coordinator with a private organisation engaged in onboard ship equipment repair & maintenance work in Mumbai.

Not finding the work assignment satisfactory, he entered into an informal venture on a 50% profit-loss basis with a company owned by his relatives, Mr Srikumar and Mr Ravi, engaged in supply of control panels and odd repair work onboard naval ships. To understand the scope of work available with various agencies Radhakrishnan spent a great amount of time in attending all seminars and exhibitions being organised by government departments and civil agencies. He soon learnt the nuances of developing and maintaining business contacts and started bidding for tenders from Navy and Coast Guards in his area of technical expertise.

Alongside, he set up his own firm and named it Linia Engineering Services. By April 1996, he was confident enough of his abilities to survive in the market, to shift his family back from Palakkad to Mumbai.

RADHAKRISHNAN SPEAKS

My first project was of merely INR 6,000 for repair of an electric motor, for which I am yet to get the payment, as I didn't maintain the procedures of submitting work orders, material entry challans, etc. My first tender, worth INR 2 Lakhs, was for supply and fitment of Fiber Reinforced Plastic

pipes for protecting cables on ships. It was out of my area of expertise, but with due diligence I handled it successfully. It gave me immense confidence.

My first year revenue turnover was INR 2, 50, 000. After a decade it rose to INR 1 crore. Today it is INR 5 crores. In 2003, I set up our company office in

Vishakhapatnam to execute business orders in that region. Today, both offices generate almost similar revenue turnover.

For five years I also tenured the appointment of Honorary Secretary of Western Region of Institute of Electrical Engineering and Technology (UK).

Learnings from the Navy

Navy showed me the importance of discipline and the need to innovate ideas and solutions to work and life problems.

Planning, mid-course corrections based on periodic review of plans and perseverance is another vital learning I carry forward from my Navy years.

There is no substitute for hands-on technical experience and confidence in self.

Navy has a multicultural workforce, necessitating emphasis on the value of soft skills and interpersonal communication in the naval leadership arena.

In business dealings I have come across three types of people, the Do Gooders, Rule Sticklers and Self-Interest predominant. Idea is to identify the person you are dealing with and read mantra accordingly.

Major Achievements

Slowly but steadily our reputation as a reliable high-quality technical service provider spread to the R&D organisations. One fine day in August 2006 we got a request for proposal for supply and installation of specified systems in a futuristic warship. We tendered and secured the order. We are now on the approved vendor list with Ministry of Defence.

In 2008, a special technology vessel under development was afflicted with a technical snag in its communication infrastructure. We were approached at short notice to execute fault finding, proving and commissioning of the system. It was a feather in our cap and also enabled us to further enhance our technical understanding of future requirements.

Today we are the sole quality providers for specified submarine systems, sole manufacturers of indigenous pneumatic valves in special naval armaments and the Business Associate of choice of R&D organisations in specified equipment.

Future Vision

We are looking at diversifying into marine engineering products and introduce IP based latest technology into onboard ship Inter-Communication systems.

Indigenous development of communication systems to substitute imported systems at almost half cost differential has already commenced.

Planning is on to double our annual revenue turnover in the next 3–5 years and expand our enterprise reach pan maritime India in West Bengal, Tamil Nadu, Kerala, and Goa, apart from Mumbai and Vishakhapatnam.

My son Rohit has joined me in Linia after his MBA in marketing, equipped & ready to take the organisation to the next level of quality and growth.

My daughter Ritu, after completing her BA (Joint Honours) in Arts & Festival Management and Dance from De Montfort University, Leicester, UK, is ready to launch her own dance theatre group "Ittha Dance Theatre" to produce, direct and choreograph onstage dance theatre performances.

Advice for the Mad Vets

I would like to impress on four points for the guidance of the veterans.

First, plan four to five years in advance of leaving the forces, shortlist suitable choices that are available for your skill sets and interests and commence preparations accordingly.

Second, to be successful entrepreneurs you have to change your thought process in alignment with the corporate world.

Third, liasioning skills are dependent more on your life skills than on your technical expertise and knowledge.

Last, your dedication today will be recognised tomorrow. Be the recognised master of your trade.

The forces veterans need to look beyond the traditional forte of providing security services. The scope to do business in services sector is vast, especially in lesser populated towns, where your reputation matters to prospective customers. The assumption that services personnel are not cut out for running own business enterprise is based on false presumption.

So select your field of business, learn all that you can about it, practice it and then execute the plan.

Options for the Mad Vets to Undertake New Ventures

Veterans have the advantage of having a steady source of income from pension, adequate availability of time on hand, generally good health, proficiency in different languages, exposure to different cultures and most importantly soft skill experience to deal with a 'gate keeper' & with the 'CEO' of an organisation appropriately and with the same ease. These all should enthuse him to dare to launch his own venture, with minimum financial risk and external assistance.

Providing maintenance and repair services is a very vast sector and very suitable for the forces veterans due to their inherent organisational skills and reliability.

Logistics Suppliers is another field very apt for the veterans.

Philosophy Towards Life

Add value to others to succeed. It will return to you.

Personal Qualities that Have Helped

Petya Class of boats are hard task masters. It is there that I imbibed personal qualities of discipline, dedication and determination.

The Future of India

India has very strong traditions and customs, including in the field of trade and commerce. There is no need for us to imitate foreign culture and ethics. For India to attain its rightful place in the world stage we have to first get over our petty infighting.

There is no stopping India, and I see a very bright future ahead for our country.

One Mantra for the Mad Vets

Do what you like and not because it will make more money.

Willingness to Mentor Mad Vets

It is my desire that veterans come in more and more numbers to start their own business ventures. I am more than willing to mentor veterans even to the extent of providing opportunities, if feasible.

On Role of Spouse

Sreelatha has inner strength and is a pillar of support for me. My father expired in 1994, just a year before I was to retire from the Navy. My well-wishers consulted an astrologer who pronounced the time as not suitable for starting business, due to influence of Shani in my astrological chart. But Sreelatha said, "We will take care of Shani, you just go ahead with your business venture." She willingly shifted with family to Palakkad temporarily to enable me to devote my full energy to the business venture.

She is a businessperson in her own right and runs her own Lia Beauty Parlor at Khargar in Navi Mumbai.

* * *

International Defense Security Projects & Services

....

The delegation-competency loop is the litmus test of leadership.
The hallmark of a competent leader is the ability to delegate, true
delegation is based on trust and trust itself flows from competency.

- Col Manbhupinder Singh Atwal

Col Manbhupinder Singh Atwal, 7 ENGINEERS, is a fourth-generation army officer. His family originally hailed from Montgomery district in West Punjab, now in Pakistan. The region straddles River Ravi and is bounded by Rivers Sutlej to the East and Chenab to its West. It lies between the districts of Lahore, Jhang, Multan, Bahawalpur and Ferozepur, and was renamed as Sahiwal in 1966. It is famous as the site of the prehistoric Indus Civilisation and for the renowned Sahiwal breed of cows. It lies along the traditional trading and invasion routes from Central Asia to India. The sturdy Jat clans, inhabiting the region, fiercely guarded their independence from both the invaders and the rulers of India, and were in a constant state of rebellion for most of the pre-British era.

His great grandfather Inder Singh was a Subedar in 1/25th Punjabis in the British Indian Army and participated in the First

World War. He was decorated with the Indian Distinguished Service Medal, the second highest gallantry medal entitled to the Indian soldiers at that time. To further recognise his service in the First World War he was granted Honorary Commission as Lieutenant in the British Indian Army and also awarded a jagir in Montgomery, Punjab, in 1920.

His grandfather Lt Nageena Singh also served with 1/25th Punjabis in the British Indian Army. The family was prosperous and owned large tracts of land in Montgomery. However, the partition of India in 1947 changed their destiny. Lt Nageena Singh was forced to flee overnight, along with his family from Montgomery, leaving behind all their possessions. He was grievously injured while bravely defending his family from the marauding Muslim mobs. Despite his injury, Lt Nageena Singh successfully led his family to safety in Adampur, District Jalandhar. He never fully recovered from his wounds and died a few years later. His youngest son got separated from the family during the partition riots and was given up for dead. Unknown to the family, he too survived the bitter journey to safety in India and got enlisted in the Bengal Sappers of the Indian Army. It was more than a year later before the family could happily rejoice being reunited with him.

His father Barindera Singh was commissioned as Lieutenant into the British Indian Army in 1944 and became the sole bread winner for the entire family comprising three brothers and three sisters. He initially served in 8 KUMAON and subsequently posted to 13 KUMAON on its raising. He was privileged to raise the Charlie Company of 13 KUMAON, with Lt Shaitan Singh as his first subaltern. During the 1962 war, Charlie Company 13 KUMAON, now ably commanded by Maj Shaitan Singh, was deployed at Chushul in Laddakh. The company entered the annals of history by fighting till the last man against overwhelming Chinese force. Maj Shaitan Singh was awarded the Param Vir Chakra (Posthumously) and the company earned the sobriquet of Chushul company. Maj Barindera Singh, as the Founding Father of the Company, took this great loss personally. He retired from service in 1966 and settled down in Jalandhar Cantt.

Early Life

Manbhupinder Singh, the elder of two siblings, was born in December 1956. Being the son of an army officer, he experienced moves from one station to another, quite often. This entailed his changing schools very frequently. The schools were often affiliated with different School Boards of Examination, having their own academic years. This anomaly twice led him to securing double promotions in a single year. As a result, Manbhupinder was a mere 14 years of age when he joined Higher Secondary Class (HSC). Unfortunately, he did not meet the minimum age requirement to appear in HSC exams.

This peculiar situation led Manbhupinder to lose interest in studies. He frequently absented from school and showed no interest in class activities. This was also the time when he started showing distinct streaks of independence and rebellious attitude towards the establishment, probably a throwback to his earlier ancestors. Manbhupinder would have easily topped the "Bad Book list," if there was one, of the school authorities. Two years down the line, in 1972, he appeared for the HSC examination and secured distinction in Physics, Chemistry, Mathematics and English in the Board examination. It was a rare feat for those times. He also topped the school. The school authorities were unable to come to terms with this record from the most unlikely student to achieve it. They went crazy trying to tally his name and roll number with the declared results before grudgingly accepting the stupendous academic achievement of their disciplinary most wayward student, Manbhupinder.

In the interim, he had quietly applied for the entrance examination to NDA, Pune. He qualified the written exams and the ensuing SSB Interview and was selected for NDA. This brought Manbhupinder to the defining moment of his life. But it would take another four years before

Manbhupinder would be able to connect the sequence of action to this defining moment.

He had already cleared his HSC Board, as well as NDA entrance exams. It was June 1972, and his training at NDA was scheduled to commence from January 1973. Manbhupinder eagerly looked forward to this interlude of nearly six months of spare time.

Maj Barindera Singh shattered his daydreams by insisting he join pre-engineering class in DAV College Jalandhar. Manbhupinder unwillingly got enrolled in the college for pre-engineering. Because of securing distinction in HSC, he was awarded scholarship in college education. Manbhupinder lacked motivation to study, because of anticipation of joining NDA within six months. His rebellious streak resurfaced, and he again started absenting from classes.

Closer to the semester examination, Manbhupinder received an official letter from Ministry of Defence, asking him to forward 'Character Certificate' prior to joining NDA. His request for the certificate was denied by the college authorities, as he had only 10 days attendance in the entire semester. In the ensuing interview with the Principal, he was advised to refund the scholarship amount before he could be issued with the 'Character Certificate.' This stumped Manbhupinder, as refunding the scholarship amount would result in the issue of poor attendance coming to the notice of his father. After fervent requests from Manbhupinder, the Principal relented. Instead he gave him the choice to sit for semester exams and pass them with good marks.

Manbhupinder studied diligently for the remaining one week, appeared in the semester exams and topped the college as well as the university. He was called by the Principal to come to his office along with his father. A nervous Manbhupinder was assured by the Principal that the issue of his short attendance would not be broached.

Manbhupinder recalls, "My father went into the Principal's office while I waited outside impatiently. After a short while my father came fuming out of the office, using offensive language. Apparently, the Principal wanted my father to withdraw me from joining NDA and, instead, join Indian Institute of Technology. Neither my father nor I were aware of IIT. We presumed the Principal was referring to Indian Technology Institute, a low-grade vocational technical training option. It was much later that we realised the true import of the advice of the Principal as well as the importance of an IIT degree. My father felt bad and later on apologised to the Principal. But the most interesting corollary to this incident came four years later, during my training at IMA, Dehradun. I approached my father for advice on choice of arms for commission. I wanted to join Kumaon or Punjab Regiment of Infantry, in deference to the regimental affiliation of my father and grandfather. My father simply stated that if I wanted to walk daily from Hoshiarpur to Jalandhar, then I should opt for infantry. But if I wanted to move in a jeep then I should join Engineers. He also highlighted that I was brilliant in technical subjects and recalled the advice of my Principal to become an engineer. That's how I got motivated to join Engineers, and the consequent course of my life changed accordingly."

Life in the Army

In January 1973, Manbhupinder joined NDA. Training at NDA is spread over six terms of six months each. Cadets are independently assessed for performance in each term, and the trainee getting distinguished grade in academics in the term is awarded with a Silver Torch. Manbhupinder achieved a very rare distinction of being the proud recipient of six Star Silver Torches in all six semesters of his batch. He passed NDA in December 1975, where he bagged the prestigious "Presidents Gold Medal" for standing first in the overall Order of Merit. But he cherishes his medal for being adjudged "Best in Drill" in NDA as the most difficult to get.

On being queried about his NDA days, Manbhupinder recalls, "The most interesting highlight of my last term in NDA was holding both the senior-most Cadet Appointments, Academy Cadet Captain (ACC) and Academy Cadet Adjutant (ACA), owing to a quirk of fate. I was originally appointed as the ACA and a few weeks before passing out date of our batch I was appointed as the ACC and another cadet made the ACA. During drill, a few of our batchmates were noticed by JCO Drill Instructors for sporting longer than regulation haircut. A Drill Instructor clipped off the frontal hair of some of the offending cadets, as a warning to others. The cadets took umbrage to this slight and took out their ire by later chopping off hairs of large numbers of junior cadets. The issue snowballed and reached the notice of Commandant who had been given the names of a few cadets responsible for this. The actions of the cadets were taken rather seriously, and I came to know that the Commandant was considering to relegate the named cadets and this alarmed me. Being the senior-most cadet appointment, I forcefully insisted on meeting the Commandant. My diligent defence and narration of the unauthorised behaviour of the Drill Instructors, as being the root cause of the incident, and the fact that many more cadets other than those named to the Commandant were involved somehow saved the day. Instead of inviting relegations, the affected cadets escaped by being deprived of their cadet appointments and other minor punishments. One of the cadets to be deprived of his appointment was the newly appointed ACA. As an interim measure, I was appointed to officiate as ACA, in addition to my appointment as ACC. As days went by, ACA was deliberately never appointed and I continued to hold dual responsibility. As per regulations, a cadet can tenure only one appointment at one time. To overcome this anomaly, the NDA Cadet Appointment Board of ACC shows my name as MS Atwal, while the ACA Board shows it as Manbhupinder Singh." This was also his first serious brush with army authorities.

His twelve-month stint as Gentleman Cadet at IMA, Dehradun was equally eventful. In his second term, Manbhupinder was given a Gentleman Cadet appointment. The Deputy Commandant wanted Manbhupinder to join the Jat Regiment, but he refused saying, "Sir, if I have to Join Infantry, I would opt for my ancestor's regiments." He was deprived of his appointment by the Deputy Commandant for allegedly wearing a non-regulation colour turban for Drill. Manbhupinder insisted on his innocence and highlighted the fact that other than the

Deputy Commandant, who saw from his office located at a distance, no one else including the drill instructors noticed it, that too when he was commanding the drill squad. But his defence was brushed aside. Probably the higher authorities later sensed something amiss, and in a rare step back, he was again awarded the Gentleman Cadet appointment. It is a tribute to his dedication and hard work, that despite this temporary setback, he passed out in the Super Block and hence commissioned into the Corps of Engineers, his first choice. It was December 1976 and Manbhupinder Singh stood ramrod erect when being pipped by his father Major Barindera Singh with the badges of rank of a Second Lieutenant of Corps of Engineers. At that instant as he recalled the sentient words of the Principal of DAV College Jalandhar spoken four years earlier that Manbhupinder would do best as an engineer, an enigmatic smile escaped his lips. He was now set on a destined course. His father too smiled back, probably with similar recall.

In January 1977, 2/Lt Manbhupinder Singh Atwal reported for duty at Madras Sappers Centre (MEG) at Bangalore. After a month, he was dispatched to CME, Pune for attending Young Officers Course. The incident at IMA had left its scars, and his brash ways perturbed his instructors enough to report the issue to the Commandant, MEG during his visit to CME, Pune. The Commandant called Manbhupinder for an informal interview. The highly experienced Commandant was able to sense the underlying rebellious streak within Manbhupinder, which could prevent him from developing his full potential and promised him a posting to the best unit in Madras Sappers. Manbhupinder took the advice to heart and began devoting his full attention to the profession.

He completed the Young Officers Course with an enviable 'Distinction' grading, a very rare occurrence. The Commandant in keeping with his word posted Manbhupinder to the then only Assault Engineer Squadron. But the Army Headquarters changed the posting to 7 ENGINEERS. The Commandant, MEG strongly objected to this change, and the matter hung in balance. The Commandant, CME was also aware of this issue and in the ceremony, for presenting the 'Silver

Grenade' to Manbhupinder for standing first on the course, asked him to think and revert to him on which unit he wanted to join. The response from Manbhupinder was instantaneous, "7 ENGINEERS, somebody in the Assault Squadron does not want me so why go there."

7 ENGINEERS was located in Chandimandir, near Chandigarh as part of an Engineer Brigade. 2/Lt Manbhupinder Singh Atwal, by another quirk of circumstance, was appointed as an officiating Brigade Major of his brigade and served in this appointment with aplomb for five months. A rare achievement for a subaltern. But he followed it up by also earning the dubious distinction of being the first subaltern from his unit to be brought before the Corps Commander for driving a military vehicle in violation of formation orders. It appeared that his brush with authorities would be an annual affair.

The Adjutant General (AG) at Army Headquarters is a principal staff officer to the Chief of Army Staff. Every year he tours major military stations to address the officers about latest policy matters and take direct feedback. In 1978 the AG came to Chandimandir to address the officers of the two Engineer Brigades located there. At that time both the formations including most of the Officer's Mess were housed in tented accommodation. During the question answer session, 2/Lt Manbhupinder Singh Atwal, probably the junior-most officer present, raised the query of the formations housed in tented accommodation in a peace station, lacking basic amenities and infrastructure such as toilets and kitchens. After hurried consultation, the AG announced time bound measures to ameliorate the difficulties by hiring private bungalows as Officers Mess, and also promised start of construction of permanent accommodation for these formations within two years.

In an interesting aside on this incident, Manbhupinder adds, "It was year 2000 and 7 ENGINEERS was again moved to Chandimandir for another tenure. I was now the Commanding Officer of my Regiment, and awaiting my move for the Higher Command Course. To my surprise I found that though basic amenities had been provided, but the promise of permanent accommodation made by AG more than two decades back had not materialised. In the next visit of the AG to our station, I had to again raise the subject with the above background. Fortunately, this time the promise made was finally kept."

Also in 1978, while participating in a major training exercise with his unit, Manbhupinder was made 'Prisoner of War' due to a misunderstanding on the 'line of control.' But he turned the tables on the exercise enemy, by overpowering his Military Police escort and 'capturing' the Redland Force Commanding General and his entourage. 2/Lt Manbhupinder Singh Atwal was commended in writing by his formation for this 'exploit.' All these incidents, combined, established his reputation of willing to work for the cause of greater good, unmindful of career interests. His reputation for professionalism had already been established by his distinguished performance on the Young Officers Course.

In 1981, Manbhupinder again moved to CME, Pune for three years to attend the civil engineering degree course. He joined the CME Rowing Club and began to practice in single Sculls. Manbhupinder was selected to the CME Rowing team for participating in the annual Regatta. Though the team lost other events, Manbhupinder won in single Sculls by a huge margin. This was to be the impetus for the subsequent domination of rowing events at CME.

While still attending the degree course, he went on to be selected for the Indian National team for SAARC Championship in 1981, won the Maharashtra State Regatta, and won the Bronze in 1982 Nationals in single Sculls. He was selected to the Indian National Team for 1982 Asian Games and attended the first three coaching camps for a total duration of three months for practising for the 1982 Asian Games and hence had to drop one semester. Due to low intake of Direct Entry Engineer Officers in the 1977 and 1978 batches the schedule for the next degree course was not certain. Manbhupinder, therefore, decided to concentrate on his career and pulled out from the national team for Asian Games.

Attending the Junior Command Course at College of Combat, Mhow holds special significance for Manbhupinder. It took a mere five minutes interaction at a social event for Manbhupinder and Jaswinder Kaur to realise that they were made for each other. The very next day they proposed and mutually accepted. They got married in 1987.

Shortly after marriage in 1987, Manbhupinder was back in CME, Pune. This time as an Instructor in Faculty of Combat Engineering, responsible for conduct of Young Officers Course. The community of the Young Officers breed is collectively the most irreverent to authority and not easily swayed by an external facade. Hence, their view speaks volumes of the professionalism and humane values of Manbhupinder.

Interacting with a small cross section of his erstwhile trainees, even after twenty years, the common recollection about Manbhupinder revolved around respect for his vast reservoir of professional knowledge, instantaneous decision-making ability, physical toughness and rowing prowess at par with his incisive intelligence and genuine approachability. He was the most sought-after guide for resolving not only professional but also personal difficulties of the Young Officers under his charge.

By now the Rowing and Sailing Clubs at CME had been overhauled and were regularly winning national and international medals in rowing. Manbhupinder shifted his event from rowing to yachting and won a silver medal each in Enterprise Class and Laser Class in the Nationals in 1987 and 1988. He went on to represent India in Laser Class in Commonwealth Sailing Championship in Mumbai in February 1987. But the most satisfying win for him was the victory of the team of Corps of Engineers over the IN team during the Nationals in 1987.

He was also selected to represent India in Laser Class in World Sailing Championship held in Plymouth, UK, and for Italy Open at Lake Garda, both in 1988. However, resource crunch delayed grant of official sanction for the move and participation in the World Championship. As a result, the team reached Plymouth just a day prior to the event and was without equipment. By the time they could organise their equipment locally, the time for registering for the event was over. From UK he went to represent the country in the Italian Open Championships in Lake Garda, Italy. On return from the trip, disillusioned with the pathetic way the national team was treated, he decided to quit sailing.

For the next three years, Manbhupinder was constantly on the move with postings at annual interval. A hectic period even from the army's normal posting interval of at least two to three years. This was also the period when he twice had close brushes with death.

With just two months preparation he cleared the prestigious Defence Services Staff College entrance examination and proceeded to Wellington, Nilgiris in Tamil Nadu for attending the yearlong course in 1989-90. On completion of the course in early 1990, he received his posting as Brigade Major in a formation headquarter deployed in counter-insurgency role in the North East. This was the first deployment for Manbhupinder in an operational area and he loved it, frequently undertaking field tasks over and above the designed role of the appointment held by him.

In the year 1920, at the time when his great grandfather Inder Singh was awarded with Honorary Commission of Lieutenant, he was also presented by the British with a .45 bore, 1919 make, Webley Mark VI revolver. The weapon was later carried by his grandfather Lt Nageena Singh during World War II and subsequently by his father Maj Barindera Singh during the 1962 and 1965 wars with China and Pakistan, respectively. It was now the turn of Manbhupinder to proudly carry this most prized family possession, while deployed in counter-insurgency operations. It was with this seventy years vintage weapon that he shot, wounded and captured the United Liberation Front of Assam 'district commander' of Jorhat. It was this weapon which he was carrying when he was shot at by the militants and a passing bullet burnt his turban, missing him by the proverbial whisker.

His tenure as Brigade Major was truncated after he was selected for deployment in United Nations Observer Mission for Iraq and Kuwait in 1991. Here again death passed him by a whisker when the vehicle used by him was blown off by an improvised explosive device. Manbhupinder reminisces, "I was heading the UN Military Observers office located in

Baghdad. We all would generally leave office at 1300 hrs for the hotel where we resided, a fifteen minutes' drive. On the given day most of the office staff had left early to attend the wedding of the sister of one of the local secretarial staff. Only I and a captain from the Austrian army remained behind to man the office. We too decided to leave office about fifteen minutes before 1300 hrs. After parking the vehicle at the hotel parking, I walked to my room. The time was 1300 hrs. Suddenly I heard an explosion from the hotel vehicle park. On rushing down, I was utterly surprised to see my official car engulfed by fire. Subsequent investigation by the police revealed that an explosive timer device had been surreptitiously fitted to the vehicle earlier."

After a year with UN Mission in Iraq, he was posted back to his unit as a Company Commander and subsequently as a staff officer at Army Headquarters. Here he was posted with Military Secretary Branch, dealing with career management of officers. Says Manbhupinder, "This was the first exposure I had to the functioning of Army Headquarters and the civilian bureaucracy, which comprised a substantial proportion of its staff. They were almost a law unto themselves. Interference in postings of army officers at the behest of bureaucracy and politicians, poorly supervised lawsuits in courts enabling sharp lawyers to prolong the legal proceedings for pecuniary gains, were all being overlooked. For the first time, I felt a sense of disquiet. Very frequently, we received requests from senior officers regarding postings, but sadly they were mostly for the professionally lowest rung of officers asking for postings to good places for personal reasons or lucrative appointments and not for grooming deserving officers. The office civilian staff advised about a rule which allowed additional increments to army personnel who had won sports medals in recognised national and international sporting events. I probably became the first officer to receive the maximum permissible five additional increments along with arrears."

In 1999, Manbhupinder was posted back to 7 ENGINEERS. He was now the CO of the unit he had joined as a 2/Lt, the most cherished dream of any officer. The unit was deployed in insurgency affected area under Headquarters IV Corps at Tezpur. The Corps Headquarters had their hands full manning the International borders and monitoring the insurgency situation within the vast Corps Zone. 7 ENGINEERS was the only Corps Troops available as a full-fledged unit in station and was tasked for Garrison Security and administration of key institutes of the station.

This was also the year when widespread floods in the River Brahmaputra devastated the Kaziranga Wild Life National Park. Manbhupinder was tasked to liaise with the park authorities for optimising assistance from the army in its resurrection. His recommendations of erecting seven dispersed high grounds, each measuring 200 mtrs length x 100 mtrs width x 20 mtrs height for providing safe islands for animals in future floods were approved. The work was professionally executed and was felt important enough to be covered by the BBC and inaugurated by the COAS himself.

Manbhupinder, the CO, was in his elements. His professional competency and daring motivated the unit to also willingly shoulder and shine in infantry operational tasks and administrative assignments. The Officers and their 'Thambis' are unequivocal in asserting, "It was our Golden Period." These five words say it all on the accomplishments of Manbhupinder's tenure as a CO.

Lt Gen SS Chahal was the Chief of Staff of Headquarters IV Corps. He later went on to be the Director General Military Operations and Commandant of the prestigious National Defence College. He says, "Manbhupinder and his versatile 7 ENGINEERS were my most precious assets. Whether it be the security of the Tezpur Garrison, engineer operational works, administering garrison institutes, civil-military liaison or rapport with influential citizens, we at the Headquarters were assured that Manbhupinder would be out with his men. This enabled us to focus our complete energy on operational tasks along the borders and countering centrifugal forces. He was professionally extremely competent and always led from the front. The best is that the troops responded to him and befittingly walked with a confident swagger."

7 ENGINEER was moved to Chandimandir in the year 2000, the station where he had first joined the unit. He had already been nominated for attending the prestigious Higher Command Course, the gateway to star ranks. The then COAS was visiting the station, just after several precious army lives had been lost in IED blasts in J&K. During an informal discussion, Manbhupinder put across a proposition for employing technical measures for prophylactic protection against IED blasts. The idea found favour with the COAS, and Manbhupinder was tasked to make a presentation to the DGMO at Army Headquarters. His proposal was approved, and the unit was allotted funds to develop the requisite equipment. The project proved to be a great success and was followed by 7 ENGINEERS being allotted funds from MOD to make the systems. Even the Ministry of Home Affairs bought four systems for use by Para Military Forces in insurgency-prone areas. The regiment co-opted Eon Infotech, a niche technology company, into the project and shared the details with them. Eon has since grown manifold and are now the leaders in India in anti-IED equipment.

He proceeded to attend Higher Staff Course at College of Combat, Mhow. The course provides exposure to higher strategy. He had good reasons to be happy with his performance when nominated to be the Blue Land Commander in a major exercise pitted at national level, wherein he received acclaim for out-of-the-box innovative planning and strategy. The choice of posting of Manbhupinder, on termination of the course, read "anywhere other than Jalandhar," and he was posted, of all places, to Jalandhar!

When posted to Headquarter XI Corps as Colonel General Staff Planning, cross-border supported terror attack took place on Indian Parliament. Op Parakram started, and the army was deployed on the Western borders in a show of force. His passion for contribution towards the operation resulted in his undertaking cross-domain functions. Col NS Bawa, then Colonel Quarter Master General, who subsequently commanded a Counter Insurgency Force and rose to the rank of Lieutenant General, narrates, "Manbhupinder's enthusiasm was infectious. Over and above his own task as Col General Staff Planning, he would assist in coordinating engineering support tasks in the entire Corps Zone, liaised with the Military Operations Directorate to get Jalandhar Cantt declared as an operational area, identified a disused plunge bath in station and on a war footing got it converted into an underground operations room, and had courage of conviction to disagree with the Army Commander on viability of certain operational issues resulting in their reappraisal."

Shortly after the calling off of Op Parakram, he submitted his resignation from service. It was a surprise decision for his well-wishers, and they initially refused to recommend it. Manbhupinder had everything going in his favour. He had secured best possible grades on all courses of instruction, tenured right career appointments, had received highest grading in his confidential reports, was the senior most in his batch and had the youngest age profile. Just the right ingredients to reach the highest ranks in the army.

Says Manbhupinder, "In the army, life outside the regiment is very distinctive from what life is within the regiment. I had thoroughly enjoyed my time with my regiment. My temperament was not suited to tenure staff appointments doing mundane paperwork. I wanted to move out before I became disenchanted. My great grandfather had joined the army in 1903, and it was 2003. Completing a hundred years of service with the army by our family was as good a time to leave as another."

On the other hand is the view of his colleagues, unequivocally put across by Veteran Lt Gen Praveen Bakshi, a former Army Commander who missed being the COAS, a 5 star Silver Torch holder of NDA, and a contemporary of Manbhupinder, "If you were to add a twist to the adage, 'No man is a hero to his valet,' by adding 'and coursemates,' it would be easier to comprehend that your colleagues who have trained alongside, day and night, over a time span of three years or so, would know your personality traits inside out. Having seen Manbhupinder from NDA days and attending selection-based career courses together, my assessment is that here's a man whose intellect is way ahead of his time, there is simply no ego, and there can be no friend to have better than him. His speed of decision making and ability to solve complex problems while standing on his feet is phenomenal. The army was unable to provide him avenues where he could demonstrate his prowess. The last nail in the coffin was hammered when he was overlooked for the appointment of Defence Attache due to extraneous considerations. As I had attended the interview alongside him, there being multiple vacancies, I can vouchsafe my statement. Manbhupinder returned from the interview and submitted his resignation. I consider the decision impulsive but that is Manbhupinder for you. With hindsight I add that he has had no cause to regret his decision."

Change of Uniform

The Corps of Engineers is a highly specialised combat support arm of the Indian Army. One of its primary tasks is to enhance battlefield mobility of own fighting formations while denying the same to the enemy. In pursuance of this task, the engineers are required to construct and also demolish roads & bridges, petroleum & water pipelines, defensive earthworks & temporary habitats, helipads & airfields, bunkers & fortifications, obstacles & minefields. Proficiency has to be developed to a level where the specified tasks can be successfully executed in hours of darkness, under heavy enemy fire and in minimum specified time frame. The Combat Engineering Task Force is therefore one of the most prized components of any combat grouping of the fighting forces. The Corps of Engineers also provide the command and control elements to the famous BRO, and are its backbone. It is no wonder that innovative skills, speed in execution, risk acceptance and nerves of steel are second nature to an army engineer. These very qualities are also vital for success in the entrepreneurial sector. Having been the CO of such an outfit, with extraordinary technical knowledge and leadership skills, Manbhupinder possessed all the skill sets to perform exceptionally in the corporate sector.

On leaving the army, Manbhupinder joined as Head Defense Projects with a diversified and respected private company in Oman. After seven years he joined an UK-based MNC in 2010 as CEO, India and Oman with his office in India. As a part of his job while in India, he oversaw and completed a consultancy contract for securing remote locations of ONGC and organising electronic security systems options for the army deployed in J&K. Manbhupinder soon realised that India in 2010 was not yet ready for high-end electronic security systems and that his aspirations would not be met working for another organisation. After a year with the MNC he quit and decided to start his own venture.

Entrepreneur Projects

Manbhupinder incorporated MSA Global LLC in Oman in 2011 with his elder son Amanvir Singh Atwal as the Director with the family holding 70% of the equity. An Omani partner holding the minimum required 30% is mandatory in Oman as per law. In 2014, he followed up by incorporating MSA Global Optro Electronics Pvt. Ltd. in India in 2014 with his younger son Angad Singh Atwal as the Director. Manbhupinder is the Managing Director of both the companies.

In the words of Manbhupinder, "My sons are brilliant in their own right and were pursuing their own course. But I wanted the family to be together and yet have individual space for growth. I therefore conceived our business organisation in a way that both the sons are independent to develop their companies as per their own goals and yet be able to synergise the operations for mutual support. Amanvir is focused on business opportunities in West Asia and beyond. Angad is engaged in developing business opportunities through the 'Make in India in Defense' route."

MSA Global LLC has been incorporated in Oman as an 'excellent' grade company, the highest grade for a company in Oman. The company is organised into Electronic Security Systems and Military Products verticals. In the eight years since its inception the company has already recorded a cumulative turnover of more than USD 200 Million and has a workforce of twenty-five of the very best in their respective areas of specialisation. MSA Global LLC is also the regional partner for many reputed Defense MNCs.

The electronic security systems vertical has already executed orders for design, installation and integration of electronic security systems to the tune of over 150 million US Dollars over the last six years. The projects under execution are valued at over US Dollars 70 million.

Military Products vertical has conceptualised, designed and delivered high mobility military weapon systems and high-end Military Communication systems of approximate value of over 80 million US Dollars.

MSA is proud of having driven a very large Military Security Systems Project of over 800 million US Dollars awarded by MOD Oman to Engineer Projects (India) Ltd (EPI), a Government of India commercial entity, and helped them execute the project. In a rare gesture, the Ministry of Defense of Sultanate of Oman in their letter, dated 23 June 2015, addressed to the Ambassador of India have commended Col MS Atwal (Retd) for his extraordinary effort in conceptualising and driving the project to successful fruition.

MSA Global Optro Electronics Pvt. Ltd. has successfully set up a state-of-the-art manufacturing facility in Bangalore, as part of its effort to participate in the 'Make in India' projects. The facility is equipped with 3D-scanning infrastructure to create manufacturing drawings enabling reverse engineering of ancillary parts. In the first phase the company focus is to actively engage with Army, Navy, Air Force and major PSUs for manufacturing ancillary parts for vintage Russian equipment and also develop enhanced quality and cost-effective indigenous substitutes for imported equipment. The company is still in a nascent stage of development but is already making a mark for itself by being shortlisted for some key projects.

Manbhupinder has always nurtured an underlying dream to do something more for India. The announcement of the 'Make in India' policy attracted him to realise his dream. He began planning to open a manufacturing hub and use it to attract collaborative manufacturing ventures with major MNCs. This project, closest to the heart of Manbhupinder, also turned out to be his Achilles Heel. In 2015, Manbhupinder invested Rs 45 Crore in a partnership stake in an Ahmedabad-based LLP (Limited Liability Partnership) company with a view to actively participate in 'Make in India' business opportunities. Unfortunately, the original partners misappropriated the money remitted by him.

Two traits characterise the psychological profile of Manbhupinder. The first is his propensity to help others. "Manbhupinder is a fantastic person who is ever willing to help his business associates, contract or no contract," says a senior official from a PSU engaged in collaborative business venture with MSA Global LLP. Lt Gen Praveen Bakshi adds, "There is no take in his acts of philanthropy, just give. Recently I had informally discussed the case of the son of an army officer who was looking for sponsorship to participate in World Rifle Shooting Championships. Manbhupinder took a mere half an hour to decide affirmatively and another twenty-four hours to transfer the sponsorship funds, and to everyone's surprise he had just doubled the required sponsorship amount."

The second and even more pronounced trait is to stand firm in adversity, especially when he feels he has been wronged. No challenge is too strong for him to confront. Some of his subordinates, who have served during his command tenure with 7 ENGINEERS, say, "Col Manbhupinder commanded the unit deployed in counter-insurgency role. The unit has yet to come across a more tenacious, unorthodox and daring CO, and he is equally at ease with himself whether in the company of senior-most officers of the army or with the junior-most troops of the unit. There is simply no question of his taking any incident lying down where he or his troops have been wronged."

Lt Gen Praveen Bakshi, when asked to comment on difficulties of Manbhupinder in the Ahmedabad-based LLP, adds, "It is difficult to pull a heist on an individual of the caliber of Manbhupinder. He is used to the clean business environment prevalent in Oman and not used to the murky wheeling and dealings in the much more complex business environment prevalent in India. He is used to giving and begetting trust. Investment in the LLP was an impetuous decision and he went in alone without advice, as the subject of 'Make in India' was very dear to him. He genuinely wants to do something big for his country."

Manbhupinder is sanguine in saying, "I have faltered in oversight on my investment in the LLP. I implicitly trusted the high intermediaries whom I presumed had a reputation to defend. Nevertheless, I am committed to pursue the wrongdoing to me to its legal conclusion. My investigations have gathered evidence by following the money trail, and I have already apprised the highest authorities about facts, as it impacts the enabling environment for the ambitious 'Make in India' policy. The case has been complicated by investment of the illegal proceeds across various states. Criminal complaints have been lodged against those involved and the cases are now under various stages of the legal process ranging from investigation to arbitration. The movement in the legal process is proceeding at a very slow pace, and has angered me on how genuine citizens are harassed by the pathetic way in which police and legal proceedings are conducted in India."

Again, the general consensus is that Manbhupinder will deploy requisite resources to win the legal battle and will move heaven and earth till the case comes to a logical conclusion. Entering the political arena for pursuing justice is also an option.

While talking about his vision for his entrepreneurial ventures, Manbhupinder says, "We shall continue to focus on the 'Make in India' through MSA Global Optro Electronics Pvt. Ltd. We also intend to expand our geographical footprint into European and US markets."

MANBHUPINDER SPEAKS

Learnings from the Army

I was brought up by my father on stories of officers of the Old Army where character, honour, trust and justness were the touchstones for defining success.

I joined the NDA at an impressionable age of 16 years and left at the age of 47 years. Whatever I am today and whatever I have learnt in life is mostly from my thirty years stay with the army.

To me the capability of a well-led organisation is exponentially greater than the sum total of capability of its individuals. The leadership quotient of the officers/managers makes a big difference. But in the ultimate analysis it is the CEO/Commanding Head who makes and mars the success of an organisation. The graph of a unit moves up and down based on the quality of its command/leadership.

In a large organization, the directive style of command is a key imperative to continued success, and this is based on the ability to delegate. The delegation-competency loop is the litmus test of leadership. The hallmark of a competent leader is the ability to delegate, true delegation is based on trust and trust itself flows from competency.

I have learnt to be averse to 'Yes Men,' even if competent. They have simply no role in my organisation.

Philosophy Towards Life

I practice purity of thought, and have an attitude of live and let live. I tend to believe everyone and respect others' views. But when a battle is thrust upon me, I fight back with full fervour.

Personal Qualities that Have Helped You

Faith in my capabilities.

Willingness to take calculated risks and tough decisions.

Learning from own mistakes and finding a way to reverse any adverse situation.

Difficulties and Overcoming Them

There is no excitement in life without difficulties, which basically arise from the tendency to do different things and overcome resistance to change. But it is the response to adversity which defines an individual.

My biggest difficulties arose when I nosedived into a project close to my heart. But I have learnt lessons. I have not let it halt my entrepreneurial expansion. Innovative planning, regular reviews and mid-course corrections have been undertaken to continue our journey.

It is my routine to spend the first two waking hours alone, immersed in my thoughts, evaluating options, strategising and planning future actions.

Impacting Life of Others

I have worked at and have been able to influence my subordinates and close family members in learning to delegate and trust in subordinates. I have also helped them in making life-changing decisions for the better.

Today large numbers of these personnel are either working for me or were provided help in successful placements in different domains.

Three Major Achievements

I have built a world-class team of twenty-five people working with me in MSA. They are the best in their respective domains, and I can trust them to deliver best-in-class results.

I have been instrumental in driving INR 5000 crores project to Engineers Project India Ltd. This is India's first defence security systems project abroad.

MSA Global LLC, in its infancy, successfully designed and delivered, within two years, an Electronics and Communications project and a Military Systems project with a combined value of INR 750 crores.

Advice for the Mad Vets

The two top ranked qualities for entrepreneur role are learning to be competent and taking calculated risks, keeping your mind open to change.

To succeed you must develop faith in yourself and trust in your subordinates. So, select your manpower judiciously. 'If you pay nuts you will get monkeys.' Getting competent and loyal people is a critical requirement.

There is a huge difference in military life and the corporate environment. Understanding this difference is vital. As a military veteran used to believing in the word of mouth you must be wary of your business associates and also of the system when you step into the civilian world. Promise definitely does not end in delivery.

Nation Building Options for the Mad Vets

First of all, sit down and think about what you enjoy doing. Then just do it.

Never change your ethos. The middle class is equally tired of the rampant corruption in the system and look at armed forces as the last bastion. So, don't belie that trust.

Enter into entrepreneur fields where there is maximum trust deficit.

Veterans should also enter as entrepreneurs in defense-related ancillary industry. Abroad, 60% defence industry is dominated by Veterans. Our armed forces need to understand this factor and should promote veterans aggressively.

'Make in India' presents excellent entrepreneurial opportunities. Start with small-scale ancillaries in your area of expertise. To start with become sub-contractors for bigger firms as you may not prequalify for many direct tenders.

The Future of India

The Indian Elephant will continue to gather pace, despite weak governance structures. Even on this front the things are improving. Bureaucratic and economic reforms need to be speeded up.

Our country is young and so are its people. Parents go out of their way to get their children the best possible education. This large educated young workforce is our biggest strength.

The working class overall has retained its values and is reliable.

The fabric of our society is very strong due to our rich culture and strong family bonds. Notice our response to Covid-19 virus pandemic.

New Era companies like TCS, Wipro and Infosys and some reputed family-owned businesses are success stories with their strong ethos based on Indian values. Their values-based success should be the role model for the Mad Vets as well as the next gen business leaders.

India is well on way to be the next success story; despite all the adversities we face.

One Mantra for the Mad Vets

Dream High with open eyes to decide where you want to be, have the self-confidence to reach your chosen objective and then enjoy doing what you have to do.

Willingness to Mentor Mad Vets

Yes. In fact, I have already assisted in launching second life careers of forty-odd Veterans, within India as well as abroad.

On Role of Your Spouse

Since the days of our grandfather, the family has followed the principle of a well-demarcated line between profession and family life. The ladies of the family do not interfere in the profession, and the menfolk accept the primacy of the ladies in affairs of the home. Bringing work to home is a strict no-no. With the changing times ladies are now welcome to join the family business and contribute. The line between work and family is still sacrosanct.

Jaswinder seamlessly slipped into her new role in our family. She is an MSc in Botany and enjoys gardening. She has also taught in school in a remote area for a couple of years.

She keeps herself fully engaged in looking after our household and family responsibilities. We are a large extended family and maintaining social relationships is in her domain. This is a huge load off my back, as I happen to be the son of eldest brother of our extended family.

We have taught our children how to spend, appreciate good things in life and take regular family holidays. We believe that once these become their "need," they remain motivated to work to earn to fulfil their needs. My view on being a successful husband is drilled down to my sons also; "ability to earn more than the wife can spend." It's a target difficult to achieve but luckily made easier by three very understanding ladies me and my sons are married to.

* * *

PART III

International Perspective

. . . .

When was the last time you truly felt happy,
Follow your passion to be happy,
Hang on to your boots to die happy.

Perspective on Veterans in United States of America: Interaction with Capt Harpreet Chaddha

"The time is ripe for putting in place an India-US Veterans Entrepreneurship Forum. The starting point can come from small but niche ventures for supplying high technology defence solutions and services and defence ancillary manufacturing through win-win collaboration of US technology lead and skilled Indian workforce."

- Capt Harpreet Chadha

Capt Harpreet Chadha has served for five years in the Indian Army as a Short Service Commission officer in the 1990s. Post release from service, he has settled in the US. Harpreet is the Chairman and CEO of Expertquote Insurance Services, a Silicon Valley-based premier Insurance Brokerage firm, alumni of Harvard Business School, and a Guest Lecturer at Stanford University. He sits on the boards of several companies like Legacy Resources Group, Veling Group, and Rhombus Power and is also on the Sheriff Advisory Board and a trustee of the Villa Montalvo Art Center in Saratoga, California.

An entrepreneur at heart, Harpreet is a charter member of TiE, a global non-profit organisation dedicated to fostering entrepreneurship and Heritage Ventures, a private equity acquisitions firm whose portfolio includes the popular turnaround success of Mexican restaurant chain 'Unamas.'

Harpreet has hosted the popular U.S. Television Segment called *Financial Fitness* that was syndicated nationally reaching 12 Million households in over 300 cities across the U.S. He is an ardent supporter of US Special Forces Veteran and California Highway Patrol 11-99.

What is the average service tenure of US armed forces personnel and average age of veterans when exiting from service, as an Officer and in below Officer Ranks, vis-à-vis India?

India has a voluntary army with 18 years colour service in the ranks, going up to 30 years based on career progression. For officers, it is from five years to forty years based on career progression and age.

US also has an all-volunteer army with a wide range of service obligations. My response does not factor the nuances of service in the US Army Reserves or the National Guard. For Soldiers, enlistment is the only path to service. An initial enlistment typically obligates a minimum of four years of active duty service, but even that can be modified to a three-year obligation with a follow on obligation of one year in the Independent Ready Reserve (IRR). Also, the obligation can be extended based on certain incentives. For instance, if a service member elects to sign a Special Forces contract at enlistment (called an 18 x-ray), he is obligated to serve six years of active duty – even if he fails in Special Forces Assessment and Selection. For officers, there are three paths. The United States Military Academy at West Point is a four year service college. Upon graduation cadets are commissioned as a second lieutenant and incur a six year service obligation. The Reserve Officer Training Corps (ROTC) is a program run at colleges throughout the country. ROTC cadets are commissioned upon graduation and incur a four year service obligation. Officer Candidate School (OCS) is a twelve week program. Enlisted Soldiers with a college degree can apply for OCS and be commissioned as a second lieutenant upon graduation.

That's a long preamble to qualify an answer. Enlisted soldiers can serve from three to thirty-two years, and officers can serve from four to thirty-four years, depending on career progression. The average service tenure for enlisted Soldiers is around seven years, and the average tenure for officers is around eleven years, with slightly higher averages in the reserve components.

Broadly what percentage of veterans take up entrepreneur roles?

The percentage of US Veterans engaged in entrepreneurship role is substantially higher due to higher numbers coming out of the armed forces because of short tours of duty. Existence of formalised institutional support is also an important incentive for influencing Veterans to engage in entrepreneurial activities.

Data on veteran entrepreneurship is limited. Only recently has there been an interest in Veterans' post-service experiences as business owners. However, there are an estimated 2.5 million Veteran-owned businesses in America. This represents 9.1 percent of all U.S. businesses. They generate about $1 trillion in receipts and employ nearly 6 million Americans, and Veteran entrepreneurship is increasing. In 2007, Veterans comprised 8.9 percent of all U.S. businesses. In 2012, the percentage increased to 9.1 percent or from 2.4 million to 2.5 million Veteran-owned businesses. When including those Veterans that are half-owners the number increases to 3.1 million, representing 11.3 percent of all businesses nationwide.

Which industry segment is preferred by Veteran entrepreneurs in US?

The Veterans in the US are primarily engaged in small-scale manufacturing, security consulting and service industries. Approximately 60% defence-related ancillary industry is dominated by Veteran entrepreneurs.

What are the institutional support incentives for Veteran entrepreneurial ventures?

There are a variety of private and public incentives for Veterans who want to pursue self-employment or start a business. Every service has its own transition program which increasingly have entrepreneurial support built in – though most of the programs are staffed by former service people with hardly any entrepreneurial knowledge or real business experience. On a larger scale, the Small Business Administration has an extensive Veteran support system, and provide preferential opportunities for Veteran start-ups. Filling the institutional gap is a virtual sea of Veteran Support Organizations (VSO). By some estimates there are 40,000 different individuals and organisations characterised as VSOs. Several are well established such as Bunker Labs, who help fledgling Veteran companies with everything from financing to planning, and other smaller VSOs like The Entrepreneurs Source provide less tangible assistance like coaching and advising. In all, there is no shortage of resources for US Veteran entrepreneurs.

There is increased commonality of national interests between India and US in the geopolitical space. The militaries of these countries have been in the forefront of promoting bilateral contacts for long. What are the views of senior Veteran leadership within these countries of establishing a Non-Government Veterans Forum to promote joint Veteran trade ventures between these countries?

Currently there is no such platform between Veterans of these countries, and the time is definitely ripe for putting in place such a forum. It will synergise the technical knowledge and skilled manpower potential available with the Veteran fraternity of these countries. The paradigm shift in India's policy of defence procurement from import to self-sufficiency through 'Make in India' provides the right opportunity for such a forum to flourish.

There is place for small but niche ventures for supplying high-technology defence solutions and services, and defence ancillary manufacturing through win-win collaboration of US technology lead and skilled Indian workforce.

The setting up of a Defence Industrial corridor is also positive news towards such jointmanship.

What Is the Way Forward to Achieve This Aim?

Host a blog for ascertaining views of the veteran fraternity at large in both countries.

Follow up with webinars between like-minded entities of these countries for generating and assessing commonality of interests.

Arrive at a decision matrix to formalise the concept.

Registration of non-profit bodies in respective countries as required by law.

VIEWS OF COL PAUL TOOLAN, VETERAN FROM US SPECIAL FORCES

Your views on establishing a Non-Government India-US Veterans Entrepreneur Forum to promote entrepreneur related contacts between veterans of the two countries?

Transition from military service to civilian employment and entrepreneurship has undergone a revolution in the last decade. To their credit, the United States Department of Defense recognises the challenges service people face when they transition out of the military and have taken significant steps to dedicate real resources to the process. Programs exist in every branch of service, and though some have matured quicker than others, they are all light years ahead of where they were 10-15 years ago.

These programs all began with the same simple goal - to help service people get a job after they leave the military. Over time, the programs have become more sophisticated and nuanced, including important elements like finding post-service purpose and decoupling from military identity. Even still, the ability of military programs to grow and evolve is challenged by their bureaucratic structure. The good news is this shortcoming has resulted in the growth of private organisations dedicated to helping service people transition. By some estimates there are 40,000 Veteran Support Organizations (VSO) in the United States today.

VSOs cover the widest possible spectrum of veteran assistance, with many dedicated to helping aspiring entrepreneurs. Anyone looking to start a venture can easily find experts willing and able to accelerate and guide their business idea, with one glaring exception. It is nearly impossible to find a VSO dedicated to guiding someone through the difficult territory of international collaboration and cooperation.

It is no secret that the business and technology relationship between India and the United States has blossomed over the last few decades. Though I am no expert, my personal experience and relationships has illuminated this reality over and over again. I can think of dozens of examples from my own study and understanding where the core of a technological innovation has been an Indian entrepreneur partnered with an American individual or interest. The symbiosis between these two entrepreneurial communities is without question.

It seems improbable then that no VSO capitalises on the commonality between Indian and American veterans with entrepreneurial aspirations.

COL Sidhu's experiment promises to bridge this gap. By creating a non-government organisation where Indian and American veteran entrepreneurs can network and collaborate, his idea promises to fast track the critical first step in a successful co-venture; building trust.

A life dedicated to service common among virtually every veteran is a foundation that supersedes most international boundaries. Even among adversaries, there is a mutual respect and admiration among professional Soldiers that transcends political and cultural barriers. In other words: Soldiers trust each other, especially among allies and friends. COL Sidhu's idea takes this natural trust and helps insinuate it into the critical first steps towards entrepreneurial success.

As the interdependence between Indian and American business grows, a place where Indian and American veterans can find opportunity and explore entrepreneurship together can only serve to make transition for both nations veterans less stressful, and more successful.

What is the way forward to achieve this aim?

Starting any endeavour to bring together like-minded veterans, whether from a common country of service or a different one, starts by building upon trusted relationships with common interests. The best way to start an Indo-American group of entrepreneurs is by getting a few who already have a relationship to be the foundation. Though an informal way to begin, it likely best to let an organisation with international aspirations grow organically instead of programmatically.

However it starts, the most important aspect is insuring the organisation provides value for its members. In this case, just providing a platform for unconventional networking would be enough, at least in the beginning. Eventually, it would likely need to expand to include some access and education about growing a joint venture with international founders, and access to venture capital and private equity firms who specialise in backing and investing in joint Indian/American enterprises.

PAUL J TOOLAN, CPD
http://linkedin.com/in/paul-toolan

* * *

PART IV

Epilogue

. . . .

Weapons cannot cleave this self,
Fire cannot burn it,
Water cannot wet this self,
Nor winds make it dry.

- Bhagwad Geeta (The Celestial Song)

My Credentials to Write On Mad

....

An empowered mind understands no fear.

Hell raising as a youngster is a run-of-the-mill affair in a testosterone-predominant environment and is generally looked at as part of growing up. It does not reflect the true leanings of individual personality.

My first serious grapple with the subject at hand occurred as a young leader. The unit had been mobilised for overseas operations and deployed sub-unit wise in spatially separated mounting bases. After a prolonged and monotonous wait, suddenly the air was abuzz with excitement and uncertainty. The word go had been received, but the quantum of effort was unclear.

To my horror, my outfit was the only one remaining in the mounting base. Before I could protest this indignity, the orders came through a special messenger to be prepared for special operations and move to the airfield at once. Para forces had taken off from a separate mounting base, and my elements were to tail them and conduct force landing in conjunction with the paras. Our excitement knew no end.

The Infantry Combat Vehicles (ICVs) were loaded and belted with ammunition in record time; such was the enthusiasm for joining active operations. We were guided to the aircraft waiting at the tarmac. Just when half of the ICVs had been loaded onto the aircraft, the Group Captain who was to fly the lead plane arrived. After visual inspection he suddenly looked at me and enquired where our ammunition load was. On being told that it was loaded on the weapons, he ordered us to unload the ammunition from the gun compartment and stack it separately in the aircraft. No amount of remonstration, as to how it would be suicidal to attempt a forced landing without weapons being preloaded, cut any ice with him. The safety of his precious aircraft was more important to him. He ticked me off by showing the price of his aircraft displayed on the fuselage. This raised my hackles, and I could not but show him the price tag of all my equipment as also the life of my men being priceless.

That was enough to be ordered off the 'craft and not to be back till we had unloaded the weapons. Considering the order impractical, and a peace time relic, I offloaded my ICVs, reversed them and moved towards a lone tree approximately 500 metres away. Since there was no communication with my controlling headquarters, I along with my men lazed in the shade of the only tree as far as the eye could see.

After a wait of approximately 45 minutes or so we were contacted by a MWO of the Air force to report back to the aircraft for loading. Apparently, the Group Captain had reported the issue to his higher ups but got ticked off by his unprofessional orders.

It was my first operational lesson, which I never forgot. You have to stand up to your own organisation for the safety of your troops.

When under heavy fire for the first time, the leading troops came under stress and reported the enemy engaging our mechanised column with a secret weapon which was spinning and emitting light. It was the quick recall, under fire, of the theory of spin stabilised projectile which saved the day from stress leading to panic. Used to seeing the projectiles only from the trigger end at field firing ranges, the first sighting of similar projectiles from the target end was the cause of identifying a "secret weapon." The sheepish smiles, and avoidance of eye contact at the close of combat, underscored the lesson that battlefield stress would always create perceptive difficulties in greenhorns and the special ability to retain sanity while all are under stress is a must have for a combat leader.

Development of a sense of humour is a pre-requisite to keep your sanity and maintain your equilibrium during prolonged operational deployment. So one could still smile while deployed on 48 hrs ambush, on being apprised over radio to be prepared to guide a VIP to the operational ambush site in broad daylight! Of course, the ambush was aborted, and the VIP received midway to his consternation!!

While interrogating a just captured militant it was revealed that they never ventured in front of a particular sector of the formation headquarter parameter. As per him whenever the headquarter defences were fired upon it invited instantaneous and prolonged retaliation from all over except the particular sector. Hence their deduction that such fire control would only be exercised by highly trained Special Forces. Discrete check on the ground revealed that particular sector being manned by a minor service unit who just went to the ground to avoid any body exposure! The impact of effective fire control on the mind of an opponent was never ever forgotten!!

I am witness to a lone militant walking at a deliberate pace across a 30 mtrs open patch approximately 100 mtrs from a post. He walked unscathed through a hail of bullets from one Infantry Combat Vehicle mounted machine gun, two Light Machine Guns and several rifles! A month later I was active participant in a fire fight wherein another militant was felled by a head shot at approximately 30 mtrs from a 9 mm pistol in a top speed running pursuit (though just a Standard Shot in pistol)!!

There is no cause to worry or panic under fire; God will do what he intends to do, so you do what you do best!!!

During an overseas deployment it was exhilarating and spirit uplifting experience to lead an operation to establish road block at extremely short notice in uncharted terrain to face off a regular unit sized force with a ragtag collection of one tenth their strength and that too with orders not to use force to avoid diplomatic incident! But of course how were the opponents to know of the "not to use force" order and were "forced' to back off!!"

The offer to take over command of 12 MECH INF (PARA MAHAR), a unit with a reputation to uphold, was accepted by me with alacrity. We got along roaringly well to the extent of undergoing a para jump cum free fall course at the young age of forty-six years, probably officer with maximum age profile then in the army, to do so. And what a struggle it was to convince the Army Headquarter mandarins that spirit of adventure can be promoted even in soldiers in their mid-forties.

After completing my command tenure, while enjoying a social evening, I found myself face to face with the then controlling officer of Army Headquarter branch responsible for career planning of Officers of my Regiment. On being asked if he could do anything for me, I promptly asked for a coveted posting to Pune in academic interest of my children. On being advised that may not be feasible, I responded in that case I couldn't care less whether I got posted to Timbuktu or Siachen. After ten days I got a call from my controlling section at Army Headquarters that there was no vacancy for a Colonel at Timbuktu so they have managed to secure my posting to Headquarters Base Camp to Siachen Glacier.

On any clear flying day the Base camp is a hustle and bustle of activity, helicopters ferrying troops and supplies, troops to be inducted into the glacier undergoing induction training at the Siachen Battle School, unscheduled heavy artillery firing, winter stocking of supplies and a myriad of activities involved in the logistics of fighting a war in the highest and most difficult battlefield in the world. Not a day goes by without display of courage beyond the call of duty, no wonder the motto is "Here great courage and fortitude is the norm." Not a day goes by without the commanders' dilemma of endangering four or more to save one. Incidents like the air drop load handler voluntarily hanging onto supply load being para dropped in the glacier just for the thrill of it, though not the norm, required sensitive handling.

Now as a veteran the opportunities to break new grounds are restricted only by the bounds of own creativity. Holding off the charge from a sounder of wild boars, lone walks in leopard infested jungles, midnight drives through crime prone interiors are definitely not for the weak hearted. In my mid-sixties, to enthuse my environment, undertook prolonged high-altitude trek, without past experience, with active support of family and friends.

And now a new cerebral activity in writing this book. The future is deliciously uncertain and all the more alluring.

* * *

Transitioning to Entrepreneurship

. . . .

Be tuned to the cosmic dance around,
So you live the present to change the future,
Change surely is the only constant in nature.

The Role of Spouse

The surest way to success and happiness in veteran life is when you live your own and your spouse's passion.

It is inherently good policy to keep the spouses of the workforce aligned to organisational needs and requirements. Firstly, a contented workforce is a productive workforce. Secondly, the spouse grapevine is capable of creating merry hell if left unmonitored, which would be detrimental for good health and functional efficiency of an organisation.

The armed forces have organisational wisdom to understand this reality. Spouses are an integral part of armed forces way of life. In fact, the integration is to the extent of buy one get one free, and an efficient ladies club secretary is more current with the goings on in the station than the military police and local intelligence combined!

So shall be the case on leaving the service. Post-service ventures, without integrating the consent of the spouse, are not conducive to good health, mental peace and happiness. Your spouse is Ministry of Defence (Finance) and Comptroller and Auditor General rolled into one. With her concurrence you cannot fail and without her approval your best laid plans shall come to nought. They know your strengths and all your weaknesses.

This knowledge is vital to them to safeguard their self-interests and like an expert judoka can floor you by pressing the right nerve.

Here it would be apt to say that even the world of spouse of the armed forces personnel is transitioning. This change commenced in the last decade of the 20th century. Today a very high percentage of spouses of the armed forces personnel are successful career professionals in the corporate sector. They are professionally highly qualified and have imbibed the discipline and work ethos of the armed forces. Their commitment, confidence and decision-making skills give them a head start over their colleagues. To that extent the transitioning of the veterans to the entrepreneur world is that much eased out, as the working spouse is available as a true partner in entrepreneurship. The independent income of the working spouse can also provide a financial cushion, to a certain extent, against the financial stress of starting an entrepreneur venture.

Managing Change

Change is the only constant in Nature. Living as well as inanimate beings, thought patterns, environment, forces of nature are engaged in the cosmic dance of change every instant. Species and individuals unable to adapt to this ever-changing cosmos are destined to be extinct. Capability to handle change per se should, therefore, be the single-most important object for continued survival and wellbeing.

We are constantly engaged in managing stressful changes in our daily life, e.g., getting up from sleep, morning chores, leaving the comfort of our house, commutation to and fro work/study/leisure and professional events. Marriage, childbirth, death of loved ones, post-retirement life/ second career, changes in our work and social support environment all have long lasting impact on our lives, and so we create elaborate support structures to help us manage these changes.

Personnel from the armed forces owing to the peculiarities of their service are prone to undergo major changes more frequently. Consequently, they have developed a unique intra organisation support infrastructure to assist them in managing these changes. Hence, one of the most stressful change which service personnel are required to confront is the disassociation from this elaborate support infrastructure at the time when they need it the most, transitioning the service to the civil walk of life. If not planned well, in extreme evolutionary term, it could be akin to cutting the umbilical cord after birth or a marine mammal having to adjust to living on land. The impact can be more stressful if simultaneously the individual is opting for a second career in the corporate industry.

Key to Transitioning as An Entrepreneur

The uniqueness of armed forces way of life is undeniable – witness the methodical deconstruct of psychological profile of trainees followed by reconstruct to suit the armed forces requirement. In a similar vein there needs to be a psychological reorientation for smooth adjustment into the corporate world.

It is but natural that there are bound to be strong **dissonances** and vital **confluences** in the functional environment prevalent in the armed forces vis-à-vis corporate world. There needs to be clarity in understanding them. Grasp of nuances to reorient self to the new professional parameters is the key to a happy and safe transition to a second career and life outside the armed forces.

Dissonance in Armed Forces/Corporate Environmental Parameters				
Serial	Parameter	Armed Forces	Corporate	Remarks
1.	Objective	Safeguarding national interest is paramount	The business of business is making money	-
2.	Guiding Principle	Winning at all cost	Maximise Return on Investment (ROI)	In war all spoils go to the victor. There is no second innings
3.	Statutory Obligations	No limit on human resource exploitation to optimise potential	Optimisation of human resource exploitation within realm of statutory laws	In the armed forces the rights are curtailed by statutory provisions

Dissonance in Armed Forces/Corporate Environmental Parameters				
Serial	Parameter	Armed Forces	Corporate	Remarks
4.	Human Resource Turnover	Guided by organisational interest	Guided by 'Free will' of the Human resource	-
5.	Hierarchy	Rigid	Need based	-
6.	Terms of Human Engagement	Non-negotiable	Negotiable	Inter-organisation freedom of movement
7.	Motivation	Appeal to higher instincts	Monetised incentives/aligned to life goals	-
8.	Organisational support structure	Comprehensive	Marginal	Dictated by harsh working environment of armed forces

Confluences of Armed Forces/Corporate Organisational Ways		
Serial	Parameter	Confluence
1.	Proficiency in Skills	Both armed forces and corporate industry skills are science in their study and art in application and demand a high level of professional competence.
2.	Human Resource Development	The two sectors accept paramountcy of developing human capital to gain that winning edge over competition.
3.	Investment in Advanced Technology	Technological lead is accepted as an essential ingredient towards maintaining competitive edge.
4.	Proactive Stance	Both accept it as a highly cost-effective strategy towards maintaining lead over the competition.
5.	Dynamic Planning	Accepted as necessary to keep pace with fast changing competition scenario.
6.	Boundary Management	Stress on boundary management to foresee opportunities and safeguard against inimical external environmental influences.
7.	Adherence to Laws	The armed forces as well as the corporate industry are answerable to their respective laws of the government.

The dissonances are the **weaknesses** of the veterans, hence the need to deconstruct veteran psychological profile and reconstruct the same in tune with the environmental parameters followed in the corporate sector. On the other hand, the organisational confluences are the **strengths** of the veterans and need to be leveraged. This is the key to the adjustment process from armed forces to corporate sector.

Learnings for Entrepreneurship Journey

To ease the path for the entrepreneurship journey for the new wave of entrepreneurs the common learnings and processes from the entrepreneur journey of our ten Mad Vet Karma Yogis are summarised below.

➤ Acceptance of financial risk is the first step of entrepreneurship.

➤ Take your dependents into confidence and secure finances for them.

➤ Support of the spouse, preferably as a business partner, is a force multiplier.

➤ Ethics and trust are your strong points, and they still command a premium in both traditional and new age business.

➤ Passion is the key to unlock your potential; identify your passion.

➤ Select your enterprise with great care; it should be money making aligned to your life goals and your passion.

➤ Believe in yourself, but discard your belief of know all and done all.

➤ Acquiring knowledge is a must; be humble to seek and imbibe knowledge afresh.

➤ Plan and strategise the selected project minutely; think through likely contingencies.

➤ Conduct pilot project(s) to gain hands-on experience and identify meeting points with your strengths.

➤ Failures will happen; be prepared to withstand initial failures.

➤ Be prepared to innovate and cut losses through mid-course corrections.

➤ Perseverance is the key.

➤ Invest in quality human resources, so hire judiciously.

➤ Share your success with your team.

➤ Trust others but maintain over watch, as trust does not always beget trust.

✳ ✳ ✳

A Karma Yogi

· ·

Passion and devotion to work is the real Karma Yoga and is really the path to our material development and spiritual salvation. Passion in our work generates self-motivation and leads to contentment and joy in daily life. Enumerated below is a *puranic* tale often narrated by my grandmother in my childhood, highlighting the power of Karma.

There was once an ascetic who commenced meditation under a tree for achieving supernatural powers. One day, while meditating, the ascetic's *samadhi* was disrupted by the droppings of a bird, which fell on his matted head. The ascetic looked up in anger, and as his eyes fell on the offending bird, it got burnt to ashes. The ascetic was amazed and overjoyed at the powers that he now enjoyed.

As per his ritual the ascetic went to a nearby village to beg for alms to feed himself. He knocked on a door and asked for alms. A young housewife, alone in the house, was breastfeeding her child. She asked the ascetic to wait while she breastfed her child. Later she poured some grains in a utensil and opened the door to offer it to the ascetic.

The ascetic was annoyed at the temerity of a mere housewife to make a yogi, possessing supernatural powers, to wait. In his arrogance he stared with angry and blazing eyes at the housewife. The housewife withstood the glare of the ascetic and with folded arms paid obeisance to him and offered the utensil containing grains to him. She then serenely looked the ascetic in the eye and said, "O lord, do not stare at me thus. I am not a bird who will get burnt by your anger."

On hearing this, the ascetic stood dumbstruck, because no one other than him knew of the incident. He immediately sensed that this mere housewife was in fact a Karma Yogi. By sheer dint of her passionate commitment to her household chores and rearing her infant child she had attained enlightenment. He asked her for her forgiveness, which was readily given. Thus chastened, he retreated from the village.

MORAL OF THE PURANIC TALE

BE PASSIONATELY COMMITTED TO YOUR WORK AND BECOME A KARMA YOGI THUS PURSUING YOUR PATH TO MATERIAL DEVELOPMENT AND SPIRITUAL SALVATION.

* * *

About the Author

The author Veteran Col RS Sidhu, 65 years, has the right credentials to write on the subject. He has served in the army for 29 years, is a decorated war veteran and post retirement has worked for more than a decade in the Education/Hospitality/Corporate Life Skills & Leadership Training sectors.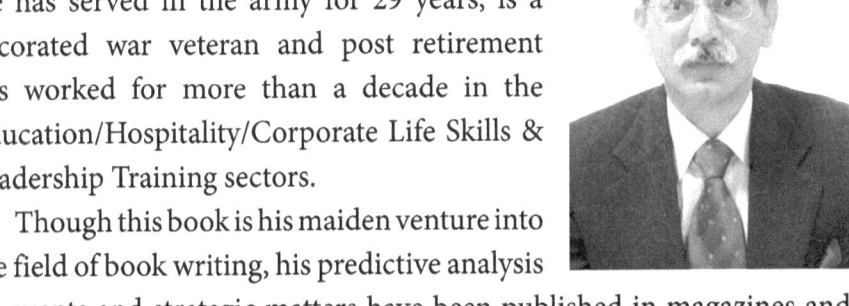

Though this book is his maiden venture into the field of book writing, his predictive analysis on events and strategic matters have been published in magazines and journals of repute.

He enjoys yoga and deep meditation and is passionate about offbeat adventures.

www.ingramcontent.com/pod-product-compliance
Lightning Source LLC
Chambersburg PA
CBHW021357210526
45463CB00001B/130